HOLY GOD—HOLY PEOPLE

Holy God—
Holy People

Holiness in Matthew, Mark, and Luke

by
W. E. McCumber

BEACON HILL PRESS OF KANSAS CITY
Kansas City, Missouri

Copyright 1982 by
Beacon Hill Press of Kansas City

Printed in 1972 under the title
Preaching Holiness from the Synoptic Gospels

Cover by: Crandall Vail

ISBN: 0-8341-0779-1

Printed in the
United States of America

DEDICATION

To George Howard Melton,
brother in Christ, colleague in
the ministry, and benefactor by
numberless kindnesses, I affectionately
dedicate this book.

CONTENTS

PREFACE

The following chapters explore the subject of holiness in the Synoptic Gospels, with special concern for the preaching values therein.

The one text of scripture, found in both Testaments, that is basic to any understanding of holiness is, "You shall therefore be holy, for I am holy" (Lev. 11:45; see 1 Pet. 1:16, RSV). This is the demand and promise of the God who redeems His people and enters into covenant with them. Therefore I have examined the subject under two categories: (1) A Holy God, and (2) A Holy People. And I have given attention to the Old Testament roots of the New Testament concept, and to its significance as covenantal.

The precise list of passages that I have considered would, no doubt, be altered by anyone else writing on this subject, by both additions and subtractions. I do not pretend to have exhausted the subject, nor to have treated it profoundly. The material presented herein lies somewhere between the hard, sweaty, painstaking task of exegesis, and the harder, sweatier, more painstaking task of preaching biblically.

As I wrote, I recalled a question asked by a certain pastor who sat beside me one day as we listened to a seminary professor lecturing on preaching. The professor referred to A. M. Hunter as "that great epitomizer of doctrine." The pastor, whose formal education had been somewhat limited, leaned over to me and asked, "What did he accuse that feller of?" I have tried to keep that pastor in mind in these pages!

9

ACKNOWLEDGMENTS

The author is grateful to the following publishers for permission granted to quote from the works named:

B. Herder Book Co., St. Louis. *Agape in the New Testament*, 1963.

Beacon Hill Press of Kansas City. *Beacon Bible Commentary*, vols. 6 and 7, 1964, 1965.

Broadman Press, Nashville. *The Broadman Bible Commentary*, 1969.

Charles Scribner's Sons, New York. *The Parables of Jesus*, 1963.

Harper and Brothers, New York. *A Commentary on the Gospel According to St. Matthew*, 1960.

MacMillan Co., New York. *The Cost of Discipleship*, 1949.

Oxford University Press, England. *A Companion to the Bible*, 1958.

SCM Press, London, England. *The Gospel According to St. Mark*, 1959.

The University Press at Cambridge, England. *The Teachings of Jesus*, 1948.

The Westminster Press, Philadelphia. *A Pattern for Life*, 1965.

Wm. B. Eerdmans Publishing Co., Grand Rapids. *Commentary on the Gospel of Luke*, 1956; *The Gospel According to St. Matthew*, 1961; *The New Testament Development of Old Testament Themes*, 1968.

11

PART ONE:

HOLY GOD

"I the Lord am holy."

I

The Holy Birth

She was found to be with child by the Holy Spirit (Matt. 1:18).

The Holy Spirit will come upon you, and the power of the Most High will overshadow you; and for that reason the holy offspring shall be called the Son of God (Luke 1:35).

For the Mighty One has done great things for me; and holy is His name (Luke 1:49).

In the Annunciation of Gabriel and the Magnificat of Mary, recorded in Luke 1, three names or titles occur which are significant for an understanding of the concept of holiness. The Father is called "holy"; the Son is called "the holy offspring"; and the Spirit is called "the Holy Spirit" (vv. 35, 49). This last designation also appears in the birth narrative of Matthew (1:18). Let us examine them all.

15

1. "Holy"

Mary exclaimed to Elisabeth, "The Mighty One has done great things for me; and *holy is His name.*" She was referring to "the Lord," whom she also designates as "God my Savior," and in whom her spirit rejoiced.

"Holy is His name." What did she mean by that? To understand Mary's terms we must go to Mary's Bible, the Old Testament.

In the Old Testament the name of God is equivalent to His *nature.* God *is* what He names himself. Thus, for instance, Jeremiah says, "Thou art great, and thy name is great" (Jer. 10:6). That God's name is holy, therefore, is to say that God is holy (cf. Lev. 20:3; Ps. 103:1; 111:9; Ezek. 20:39). For this reason, Isaiah can forge the description into a designation: "The Lord God of Israel" is also "the Holy One of Israel" (Isa. 1:4; 5:19; 12:6; 41:14; 43:14; etc.). It is noteworthy that in Isa. 43:3 we find conjoined all the express names and titles employed by Mary: "I am the Lord your God, the Holy One of Israel, your Savior." Thus Mary's words, "Holy is His name," are equivalent to "Holy is He." The personal nature of God, who reveals himself by means of His name, is the focus of Old Testament statements about holiness. As Eichrodt puts it, "'Holy' is the epithet deemed fittest to describe the divine Thou whose nature and operations are summed up in the divine name."[1] Therefore, holiness describes "that which is distinctively characteristic of God, that which constitutes his nature."[2]

This brings us to the question: *What does it mean to say that God is holy?*

Old Testament scholars are generally agreed that God's holiness means, first of all, His *utter transcendence,* "the

---

1. *Theology of the Old Testament* (Philadelphia: Westminster Press, 1961), 1:273-74.
2. Ibid.

absoluteness, majesty, and awfulness of the Creator in distinction from the creature."[3] "I am God and not man, the Holy One in your midst" (Hos. 11:9). He is the Holy *One;* no other is holy in fully the same sense as is He! He is "the wholly other, the incomprehensible, the unanalysable, the unfathomable."[4]

Yet His otherness is not remoteness. His transcendence is not distance! He is "the Holy One in your midst." The transcendent God is also the *immanent* God, coming to men in order to save them. The "Hymn of the Red Sea" contains an ascription of holiness to God that blends the concepts of transcendence and immanence. God is praised as One who is unique and yet involved, who acts in history for the salvation of men. "Who is like thee, O Lord, among the gods? Who is like thee, majestic in holiness, terrible in glorious deeds, doing wonders?" (Exod. 15:11).

Just as the Exodus becomes the basic model for the Old Testament understanding of redemption, so it furnishes the idea that divine holiness is associated with God's intervention in history to effect the deliverance of His chosen people. The Holy One is not a cold, aloof spectator of human affairs. He enters into the lives of men in order to bring them into His life. "Yahweh is holy inasmuch as He imparts Himself, inasmuch as He wishes men to share in His own divine life. . . . His holiness . . . confronts man to pour out upon him a new life."[5]

To the ideas of essential otherness and redemptive involvement we must add that of *moral perfection.* Holiness, applied to God and men, has an ethical quality. God's holiness is the antithesis of, and is antagonistic to, all moral

---

3. J. C. Lambert, "Holiness," *International Standard Bible Encyclopaedia* (Chicago: Howard-Severance Co., 1915), 3:1403.

4. P. Bonnard, *A Companion to the Bible,* ed. J.-J. Von Allmen (New York: Oxford University Press, 1958), p. 166.

5. Ibid.

pollution and stain. "There is a moral quality in the holiness of God as well as the numinous quality."[6]

It is the moral quality in God's holiness that caused Isaiah to become conscious of his sin and fearful for his life in the presence of the holy Lord (Isa. 6:1 ff.). Beholding the Lord exalted in holiness, hearing the seraphim solemnly chanting the Trisagion, the smitten prophet exclaimed, "Woe is me! . . . I am a man of unclean lips . . . my eyes have seen the King, the Lord of hosts!" In the vision of the Lord "high and lifted up," we see the element of transcendence and the numinous effect it produces. In the response of grace to the prophet's despair, that is, in the fiery coal from the altar and the pronouncement of cleansing, we see the element of immanence expressed as redemptive concern. But the main thrust of the passage is the element of moral perfection which exposes sin and makes it intolerable. Vriezen is correct in affirming that Israel knew the Holy One "as the absolutely Moral God, who will not compromise with anybody in any province of life when justice and truth are at stake."[7]

"Holy is His name," exclaimed Mary. By this she meant, He is the transcendent, redeeming, and moral One. This God confronted and elected her to bear the Man who would be the revelation of His holiness in its fullest, truest form.

2. "Holy Spirit"

From the Old Testament, Mary would understand the Holy Spirit as "the power by means of which God acts."[8]

---

6. H. H. Rowley, *The Faith of Israel* (Philadelphia: Westminster Press, 1956), p. 66.

7. *An Outline of Old Testament Theology* (Wageningen, Holland: H. Veenman & Zonen, N. V., 1960), p. 161.

8. Ph.-H. Menoud, *A Companion to the Bible*, p. 168.

He is "the power of the Most High" exercised at the point where God acts for and upon the world and man. The Hebrew word for spirit *(ruach)* is from a root meaning wind, storm, or breath. As applied to God, therefore, "the Spirit always carries with it the idea of power in which God is active."[9]

The Spirit is active in the creation of the world (Gen. 1: 2). And He "comes upon" or "possesses" men to qualify them for the work to which they have been called by God. Bezalel, for instance, is filled with the Spirit of God, and as a result he has "ability," "intelligence," "knowledge," and "craftsmanship" for the task of building and furnishing the Tabernacle (Exod. 31:1-11). By the power of the Spirit, also, the judges delivered Israel from her oppressors, renewing her independence under God (Judg. 3:10; 6:34; 11:29; 14:6; 15:14). The Spirit is also "the energy and divine intelligence which possesses the prophets,"[10] qualifying them to function as the spokesmen of God (Isa. 6:.:6; Mic. 3:8; etc.).

The phrase used by Gabriel, "the Holy Spirit," does not occur frequently in the Old Testament (Ps. 51:11; Isa. 63: 10). Perhaps Menoud is right in saying, "The adjective 'holy' adds nothing new to the noun 'spirit'"[11] for "Holy Spirit" and "Spirit of God" are one and the same. But the adjective does designate the active Power as a Power exercised in harmony with, and as the expression of, the nature of God as "the Holy One."

The Holy Spirit, then, indicates the power of *transcendence.* "Holy Spirit" is not a phrase that describes human ability raised to its highest power, but designates a power that is divine in its origin and incomparable in its effects.

---

9. A. M. Hunter, *The Gospel According to Saint Mark*, Torch Bible Commentaries (London: SCM Press, 1959), p. 28.

10. Menoud, op. cit., p. 169.

11. Ibid.

The Holy Spirit further indicates God's power in association with His *redeeming purpose*. When the Spirit empowers the judges and inspires the prophets, it is for the achievement of deeds and words by which God's intention to save is carried out in Israel and for the world.

Finally, the Holy Spirit links the mighty power of God with the *moral perfection of God*. God acts in such a way that His character is never compromised. He *does* what He *is*.

The angel proclaims, therefore, that Mary's impregnation will be achieved, not by human agency and ordinary means, but by the direct, creative, supernatural power of the Holy God. The Creator is at work in producing the "Second Man" as surely and directly as He was in making the first man. In the Virgin Birth "the procreative power of womanhood in its utmost purity united with the omnipotence of a holy and loving God." [12]

3. "Holy Offspring"

Mary's Child will be "holy" as the Creation of the Spirit and as the Revelation of God. Jesus is unique, "the Son of God," in a sense in which no other has been, is, or can ever be. Jesus is "the humanity of God," by whom the Transcendent becomes most immanent—the Holy One in our midst, *Emmanuel*. In Jesus, the eternal Word of God becomes man.

But He is not just another man, different from His fellows only in the degree of His love, power, wisdom, and God-consciousness. He is "the Holy One of God" (Mark 1: 24; Luke 4:34), the Holy because He is the One, the unique. The entire gospel tradition, by the way it applies the "Son of

---

12. Charles L. Childers, *Beacon Bible Commentary*, "Luke" (Kansas City: Beacon Hill Press, 1964), 6:436.

God" title to Jesus, "expresses the historical and qualitative uniqueness of his relation to his Father."[13]

The conjunction of "holy offspring" with "Son of God" emphasizes this uniqueness of Jesus. In the Old Testament, angels and men are called sons of God. The phrase is used of them in an adoptive sense, not a generative sense, however. They are not sons of God by reason of natural birth but by reason of gracious acceptance. Hence, in the Old Testament, individuals are *sons* of God but *not children* of God. The terminology of natural generation is usually avoided in order to distinguish Israel's God from the pagan gods who, according to mythology, had produced offspring by mating with goddesses or with women. Yahweh had no female consort; indeed, Hebrew has no word for "goddess"!

The words of Ps. 2:7 are not an exception to what I have just stated. "You are my son, today I have begotten you," refers "not to the birth of the Messianic King, but to His induction into office."[14] For this reason the words are quoted in connection with the baptism of Jesus (Matt. 3:17; Mark 1:11; Luke 3:22) but not in connection with His birth, even though He is called "Son of God" at the Annunciation. The Old Testament concept of the fatherhood of God, in the case of the nation or its king, "is a relationship into which God enters by a gracious act; to set it over against the paternity of a human father is to have recourse to an entirely different circle of ideas."[15]

That a Man is the Son of God from His birth, and in virtue of His birth, marks that Man as unique from all others to whom the epithet has ever been applied. When the

13. Oscar Cullmann, *Christology of the New Testament* (Philadelphia: Westminster Press, 1959), p. 275.

14. J. Gresham Machen, *The Virgin Birth of Christ* (Grand Rapids: Baker Book House, 1965), pp. 282-83.

15. Ibid.

New Testament refers to Jesus as "the Son of God" and to Christians as "sons of God," two different kinds of sonship are intended. "The terminology is similar, but the meanings are poles asunder."[16]

This uniqueness, this holiness of His nature makes sense of the Virgin Birth. It is logical for One so unique in His person to be also unique in His origin!

The virgin birth of Jesus also points to His holiness in the sense of moral perfection, that is, of sinlessness. He is conceived in and born from a virgin as the result of her "overshadowing" by the Holy Spirit. Therefore He is not partaker with us of racial sin. "God did a new thing in the earth when his Son became incarnate, and the virginal conception was part and parcel of that new thing. In this way, for once, the entail of sin was broken within the human family."[17] Jesus was holy, not only as the Agent of God's purpose and the Bearer of God's Spirit, but in His essential being. This sinlessness, tested and perfected in obedience to the Father's will, qualified Him to become an Offering for sin and our Reconciler to God.

This relation of the "holy offspring" to God's redeeming purpose is exposed in the name He bears: "You shall call His name Jesus" (Matt. 1:21). Jesus means, "Yahweh's salvation," or "Yahweh is salvation." "His birth is the miraculous coming of God into human life to dwell with men and save them from their sins."[18]

This means that the power of holiness is the power of love, a power that is exercised graciously. In the fine phras-

---

16. Vincent Taylor, *The Names of Jesus* (London: Macmillan & Co., 1954), pp. 69-70.

17. F. F. Bruce, *Basic Christian Doctrines*, ed. C. F. H. Henry (New York: Holt, Rinehart, & Winston, 1962), p. 129.

18. Floyd Filson, *A Commentary on the Gospel According to St. Matthew* (New York: Harper & Brothers, 1960), p. 54.

ing of Francois Varillon, His holy power is "the merciful omnipotence of love."[19]

In the virgin birth of Jesus, therefore, the *gospel* is already indicated. For here the love of God and the power of the Spirit produce a Savior, in a way that men could not produce Him, to deliver those who are helpless to redeem themselves. "This initial event, *God with us*, does not happen by chance or by natural causes or by human planning. The gospel is the story of what God has done for man's salvation."[20]

The holiness of Jesus dates from His very conception and birth. The One whose name is Holy chooses Mary to bring the Holy Offspring into the world. This is achieved by the power of the Holy Spirit. Jesus is, therefore, the Revelation of God in His *transcendence*, in His *redemptive power and love*, and in His *moral perfection*.

* * *

What does this mean in terms of preaching holiness? To preach Jesus Christ is to proclaim the Incarnation by means of the Virgin Birth. To preach the Incarnation in its significance for holiness is to view Jesus Christ as the Revelation of divine holiness. What we mean when we say that God is holy is comprehended only by looking to Jesus.

1. *We are to preach Jesus as the Revealer of the transcendent majesty of God.* Something of the mysterious "otherness" and "apartness" of God, an otherness which is not remoteness, is seen in Him. The majesty of holiness in God, which awes man and causes him to be at once attracted to and repulsed from God, attaches also to Jesus. Compare

---

19. *Announcing Christ* (Westminster, Md.: Newman Press, 1964), p. 154.
20. Filson, op. cit., pp. 54-55.

the incident recorded in Luke 5:8. There Simon Peter, made conscious of his sin in the presence of Jesus' holiness, cries out, "Depart from me!" Yet he kneels before the Lord even while saying it!

Jesus was conscious of possessing a unique relationship to God, one unshared and unsharable by His disciples. Thus He taught them, when they prayed together, to say, "Our Father." But when He includes himself with them, He always says, "My Father and your Father" (cf. Matt. 6:9; John 20:17).

The disciples were aware of this distinction. They "found in Christ a relationship to God that was absolutely unique," and expressed this conviction by the way they used the title "Son of God." Their teaching was "carried over from the usage of Jesus Himself."[21]

We preach the divine Christ or we do not preach New Testament holiness!

2. *We are to preach Jesus as the disclosure of God's redemptive concern for men.* The Holy One of Israel was, as we have seen, not the distant and uncaring One, but the Redeemer, who decisively intervened in history to judge and to save His people. And in Jesus this redemptive purpose and power comes to its fulfillment. As the Son of God who is named Jesus, He does battle with the enemies of man, overcoming sin and death. He thus provides deliverance from the bondage, pollution, and doom of sin for all who believe on Him.

3. *We are to preach Jesus as the unveiling of God's moral perfection.* His utter sinlessness makes Him the Antagonist of all that is unholy and unlovely. His antagonism to sin is more than negative recoil from evil; it is positive assault upon evil. He is the relentless Foe of all the injustice,

---

21. Taylor, op. cit., p. 69.

untruth, and hatred that mars and damns the lives of men. His life and death are a campaign against sin, which He cannot tolerate, in order to rescue man, whom He refuses to abandon. In the Mirror of Jesus, who is the Holiness of God, men can see their sin and sense their need for Him.

4. *There are distinct preaching values in the names given to Him in these scriptures.* The Virgin-born is Emmanuel, "God with us," "the Holy One in the midst." And He is Jesus, the Savior. His preaching, teaching, healing, exorcisms, death, and resurrection are military strategies by which Holiness dooms unholiness and restores men to God.

By the initial event of the New Testament, the conception and birth of Jesus, we are committed to preaching holiness, the holiness of God revealed in Jesus and provided for men!

II

The Holy Anointing

Then Jesus arrived from Galilee at the Jordan coming to John, to be baptized by him.

But John tried to prevent Him, saying, "I have need to be baptized by You, and do You come to me?"

But Jesus answering said to him, "Permit it at this time; for in this way it is fitting for us to fulfill all righteousness." Then he permitted Him.

And after being baptized, Jesus went up immediately from the water; and behold, the heavens were opened, and he saw the Spirit of God descending as a dove, and coming upon Him;

and behold, a voice out of the heavens, saying, "This is My beloved Son, in whom I am well-pleased" (Matt. 3:13-17).

PARALLELS: Mark 1:9-11; Luke 3:21-22

Jesus was born "King of the Jews" (Matt. 2:2). He was the promised Messiah-King to whom the Old Testament looked forward in such passages as Psalm 2. At His baptism in the Jordan, and with the descent of the Spirit upon Him, Jesus was anointed of God for His kingly office. Here began His ministry as the Messiah. Our task in this chapter is to review this event in its significance for holiness.

At His baptism, testimony was borne to the holiness of Jesus. This testimony embraced the three elements that we found blended into the Old Testament concept of divine holiness, namely, uniqueness, redemptive involvement, and moral perfection.

1. *The uniqueness of Jesus*

Of greatest significance here is the testimony given by God the Father. "A voice came out of the heavens: 'Thou art My beloved Son, in Thee I am well-pleased'" (Mark 1:11; Luke 3:22). The Father's words attested the unique relationship in which Jesus stood to Him. "In ancient usage, both Hebrew and Greek, 'beloved son' meant 'only son.'"[1] Jesus was thus acclaimed the Son of God in a sense not true of angels or men, but only of himself.

The baptism did not constitute Jesus the Son of God. This He already was, as we have seen, from His very conception and birth (cf. Luke 1:35). The office of Messiah did not make Him the Son of God. The Gospels do not advocate an adoptionist Christology. Rather, He is consecrated to the office of Messiah because He is the unique and incomparable Son of God. In the words of R. V. G. Tasker, "He did not *become* Son of God at His baptism. . . . It was then that

---

1. F. C. Grant, *The Gospel of Mark*, Harper's Annotated Bible Series (New York: Harper & Brothers, 1952), p. 20.

27

He was appointed to a work which He alone could perform, because of His unique relationship with His Father."[2]

We have seen earlier that this unique relationship to God is associated with the holiness of Jesus. It reflects the transcendent majesty of Yahweh, so frequently and passionately celebrated in the Old Testament. Here the one God of Israel—indeed, of the whole universe (Isa. 44:6)—declares that Jesus is His one Son, participating in His being and life as no other can. Vincent Taylor regards as the very essence of Jesus' baptism "the authentification of his filial consciousness," producing a permanent conviction "of being the Son of God in a unique sense."[3]

2. The moral perfection of Jesus

In the voice which spoke from heaven there was a tribute paid to the moral perfection of Jesus, as well as to His unique filial relationship. "In Thee I am well-pleased." These words certainly imply the sinlessness of Jesus. Later on He will say of himself, in the presence of His harshest critics, "I always do the things that are pleasing to [the Father]" (John 8:29). Here the Father sets His seal of approval on Jesus' growing-up years. So little is recorded of these years that we call them "the hidden years at Nazareth." But they were not hidden from the Father, and His righteous judgment is pronounced upon them at the baptism. As G. Campbell Morgan has written, "It was a declaration of the perfection of Jesus, and consequently of the value of that sacrifice which He would ultimately offer."[4]

---

2. *The Gospel According to St. Matthew*, Tyndale Bible Commentaries (Grand Rapids: Wm. B. Eerdmans Publishing Co., 1961), p. 50.

3. *The Life and Ministry of Jesus* (New York: Abingdon Press, n.d.), p. 60.

4. *The Crises of the Christ* (New York: Fleming H. Revell Co., 1936), p. 124.

Further testimony to the moral perfection of Jesus is given by John the Baptist. When Jesus came to John's baptism "John tried to prevent Him" (Matt. 3:14). John had thundered a call to repentance and had required a confession of sins from those who wished baptism at his hands. In Jesus, however, he discerned no such need and exclaimed, "I have need to be baptized by You, and do You come to me?" David Brown paraphrases, "What! Shall the Master come for baptism to the servant—the sinless Saviour to a sinner?" He then adds this comment: "He evidently regarded Jesus as *Himself needing no purification*, but rather *qualified to impart it to those who did*"[5] (emphasis mine).

Just how John recognized the moral perfection of Jesus we are not informed. But there is no other plausible explanation for his reluctance to perform the requested baptism. John demanded that men repent and evidence that repentance by changing their ways of living (cf. Luke 3:10-14). "When Jesus appeared before him, he made no such demand, because he saw no sin in Jesus."[6]

The moral perfection of Jesus received an incidental witness in the form in which the Holy Spirit descended upon Him—"like a dove" (Mark 1:10). The Spirit's descent upon the disciples at Pentecost was externally symbolized by *fire*, an emblem of cleansing appropriate to the impurity from which those disciples needed deliverance (cf. Acts 2:2-4; 15:8-9). At the Jordan, however, the Holy Spirit comes as a dove, an emblem of purity befitting the unstained nature and life of Jesus. "What is new and unique in Jesus is that the Spirit finds His nature utterly without anything which might obstruct His entry. . . . Jesus and the Spirit live

---

5. *A Commentary Critical, Experimental and Practical on the Old and New Testaments,* Jamieson, Fausset, & Brown, reprint ed. (Grand Rapids: Wm. B. Eerdmans Publishing Co., 1948), 5:14.

6. Frank Stagg, *The Broadman Bible Commentary* (Nashville: Broadman Press, 1969), 8:94.

and act in one perfect unity of will."[7] Into no other life has the Holy Spirit been able to make such an unobstructed entrance. Jesus was one with God in holiness.

3. The redemptive involvement of Jesus

We saw in the former chapter that holiness as transcendence and as moral perfection are linked to holiness as immanence, immanence expressed in redemptive activity. This element in the holiness of Jesus also comes into view at His baptism, because He undergoes baptism as "a consecration to the death that awaited him,"[8] a death by which sinners are redeemed.

The consent of Jesus, the Sinless One, to a baptism designed for penitent sinners can only be understood in some vicarious sense. Jesus knew himself to be uniquely the Son of God destined as the Messiah-King. But He also knew himself to be the Servant of Yahweh upon whom the sins of His people would be laid in atoning sacrifice (Isaiah 53). This is made evident by the Father's speech at the baptism. It brings together the "coronation formula" of the Messiah-King in Ps. 2:7 and the "ordination formula" of the Servant of Yahweh in Isa. 42:1. As Hunter says, "This synthesis is no accident. Here is one who knows himself to be at once the Messiah and the lowly Servant of the Lord."[9]

And if Jesus knew himself to be the Messianic King and yet the suffering Servant of Yahweh, "He also knew that His throne must be a Cross. . . . His conquest must have as its only weapon the power of suffering love."[10] In His

---

7. Menoud, op. cit., pp. 169-70.

8. E. F. Harrison, *A Short Life of Christ* (Grand Rapids: Wm. B. Eerdmans Publishing Co., 1968), p. 75.

9. Op. cit., p. 29.

10. Wm. Barclay, *The Daily Study Bible*, "The Gospel of Matthew" (Philadelphia: Westminster Press, 1958), 1:52.

holiness He does not withdraw from men, even the most depraved men; rather He enters so deeply into their lives as to take upon himself the loathsome weight of their sins, guilt, and estrangement from God. His willingness to endure that woeful burden in vicarious suffering is expressed at the beginning of His ministry by His insistence upon baptism. There at the Jordan, in consenting to be baptized, "Jesus identified himself with the people he came to save. Right at the outset of his ministry he was 'numbering himself with the transgressors.'"[11]

In this identification with sinners His holiness is affirmed, not compromised! "He had to be initiated into our sin without becoming a sinner."[12] He accomplished this in the baptism which consecrated Him to the Servant's life and death.

This life and death, this Messianic ministry, will be accomplished in the power of the Holy Spirit. As we observed in the previous study, the Holy Spirit is the Power by which God carries out His redeeming activities. Thus Jesus, the Son of God, who is to be the Savior of men, receives the Holy Spirit in measureless fullness (cf. John 3:34).

Just as the words "Thou art My beloved Son" (Mark 1:11; Luke 3:22) should not be construed to mean that Jesus became the Son of God only at His baptism, so the reference to the Spirit descending upon Him does not mean that Jesus had not possessed the Spirit before this time. Rather, the Spirit comes upon Him in a new way for a new reason—"to rouse him to action and give him power and guidance for his work. Jesus at baptism is equipped for his task."[13]

The dove emblem was beautifully appropriate, not only

---

11. Ibid.

12. C. E. Simcox, *The First Gospel* (Greenwich, Conn.: Seabury Press, 1963), p. 29.

13. Filson, op. cit., p. 68.

to the purity of Jesus, but also to the nature of His task for which the power of the Spirit is conferred. As Stagg observes, "The dove is among birds what the lamb is among animals." [14] Each of these gentle creatures was used for *sacrifice*, and Jesus "offered Himself without blemish to God" through "the eternal Spirit" in order that men might be freed "to serve the living God" (Heb. 9:14).

And so, at the baptism, testimony is borne in various ways to the holiness of Jesus, to the uniqueness of His person, to the moral purity of His conduct, and to the redeeming activity that will claim His pure life for the sake of sinful men.

* * *

What a message is here for the preacher of holiness! It might be outlined as follows:

1. *Just as the gospel was indicated in the birth of Jesus,* the holy God achieving the salvation of unholy men who could not produce their own salvation, *so the gospel is powerfully proclaimed in the event of His baptism.* Here, once again, the divine holiness embraces human sin in order to overcome and destroy it! The One who is "holy, innocent, undefiled, separated from sinners and exalted above the heavens" (Heb. 7:26), nevertheless indentifies himself with sinners by consecrating himself to a sin-bearing death on their behalf. Thus, in Him with whom the Father is well pleased lies the hope of us all with whom the Father is justly displeased. This good pleasure is declared just when He has taken the sinner's place! In this we are assured of forgiveness and acceptance with God through faith in Jesus!

2. An important lesson is here, also, for the disciples of Jesus, who are called to be in the world, yet not of the world,

---

14. Op. cit., p. 95.

and yet for the world. *In His example we see that moral purity is not preserved by isolation from men!* Rather, it is expressed by involvement with men at the very point of their sin and guilt and hunger for God. We do not protect our holiness by repudiating sinners from a safe moral distance! On the contrary, we invest it by identifying with them for the sake of their salvation. At the cost of being wounded and even killed by the sin we hate, we are to seek and serve the world He loves!

3. *Our service to human need cannot be rendered in the energy and enthusiasm of the flesh.* Jesus, holiest of all in character and behavior, yet needed special anointing for His task. How much more do we moral defectives require the Spirit's infilling if we are to serve our generation by the will of God! Not by the efficiency of our organization, nor by the cleverness of our programs, can we reach men for God. Only in that indefinable and indispensable presence and power of the Holy Spirit can the work of the Kingdom be accomplished. The descent of the Spirit, now as fire, to purify and energize our inner lives, is our only adequacy as the servants of the Servant of God. But in the fact that He receives the Spirit without measure, we are assured that He also can give us the Spirit to the measure of our capacity to receive Him.

4. *The Holy Spirit equips us to serve men, not to rule them; to minister and not to manipulate or master people.* The Spirit is Power, but He is the Power of that divine holiness which is manifested in the redeeming sufferings of Jesus Christ for undeserving sinners. The form of the Church in this age must be the servant form, and its service must involve a patient, suffering, and forgiving love reminiscent of the attitude and action of Jesus Christ. Holiness is the power of love, the power of the basin and towel, the power of the Garden and the Cross. These are the imple-

ments of Him who reigns, not as a Messiah for whose portrait a Caesar might pose, but as the Messiah whose portrait was drawn in the sufferings of the Servant of the Lord in Isaiah 53. Only as the Holy Spirit comes to destroy our ego-centricity and to empower a service-oriented life can we truly be the holy people of the holy Lord.

We must bring our hearers to the Jordan to see Jesus baptized if they are to grasp the full meaning of holiness! This unselfish, vicarious, and triumphant identification with the "lowest, least, and lost" must be seen as our hope of deliverance from sin and our pattern of service to men.

This means, first of all, that we must go to the Jordan ourselves! Jesus was not permitted to embark upon His Messianic career until He was anointed with the Holy Spirit. Then His followers were forbidden to launch their distinctive gospel vocations until they had been filled with the Spirit from on high. The lesson is too obvious to miss!

III

The Holy Ministry

A. Holiness Tested

Then Jesus was led up by the Spirit into the wilderness to be tempted by the devil.

And after He had fasted forty days and forty nights, He then became hungry.

And the tempter came and said to Him, "If You are the Son of God, command that these stones become bread."

But He answered and said, "It is written, "MAN SHALL NOT LIVE ON BREAD ALONE, BUT ON EVERY WORD THAT PROCEEDS OUT OF THE MOUTH OF GOD.'"

Then the devil took Him into the holy city; and he had Him stand on the pinnacle of the temple,

and said to Him, "If You are the Son of God throw Yourself down; for it is written,

'HE WILL GIVE HIS ANGELS CHARGE
CONCERNING YOU';

and

> 'ON *their* HANDS THEY WILL BEAR YOU UP,
> LEST YOU STRIKE YOUR FOOT
>> AGAINST A STONE.'"

Jesus said to him, "On the other hand, it is written, 'YOU SHALL NOT PUT THE LORD YOUR GOD TO THE TEST.'"

Again, the devil took Him to a very high mountain, and showed Him all the kingdoms of the world, and their glory;

and he said to Him, "All these things will I give You, if You fall down and worship me."

Then Jesus said to him, "Begone, Satan! For it is written, 'YOU SHALL WORSHIP THE LORD YOUR GOD, AND SERVE HIM ONLY.'"

Then the devil left Him; and behold, angels came and began to minister to Him (Matt. 4:1-11).

PARALLELS: Mark 1:12-13; Luke 4:1-13

At the risk of being repetitious, let us glance back over the ground we have so far traveled.

Taking our clues from the Old Testament, we have defined the divine holiness as: (1) transcendent majesty, God's otherness from His creatures; (2) immanent mercy, God's redemptive involvement on behalf of His people; and (3) perfect morality, God's freedom from and antagonism to all that is evil.

This holiness we have seen revealed in Jesus at His birth. (1) His "otherness" is linked to the title "Son of God," which marks His distinctively unique relationship to the Father. (2) His involvement is associated with the name Jesus, which means Savior. (3) His sinlessness is attested by His virginal conception and birth as "the holy offspring."

Further, this divine holiness is disclosed at His baptism. (1) His uniqueness is affirmed by the Father's words from heaven. "This is My beloved Son." (2) His redemptive concern is seen in the fact that, although sinless, He comes to the baptism for sinners, identifying himself with their profound need. (3) His sinlessness is witnessed by the Father, who said, "In Thee I am well-pleased" (Mark 1:11; Luke 3:22); by John the Baptist, who shrank from baptizing One so morally superior to the baptizer; and by himself, in His very omission of any confession of sins, which others were making, when He was baptized.

Now this Jesus, the Son of God from birth, anointed as the Servant of the Lord at His baptism, undergoes an excruciating experience of temptation in some unidentified "wilderness." The Spirit came upon Him at the Jordan and "immediately impelled Him to go into the wilderness" (Mark 1:12). There He was "tempted by Satan." Matthew and Luke inform us that He was "led" by the Spirit, but Mark's term is stronger—"driven" (KJV) or "impelled" (NASB). This does not point to any resistance on the part of Jesus. Rather, it shows, as Harrison points out, that "the initiative was on the side of the divine and not of the diabolical."[1] Jesus was not "cornered" by Satan. He moved to meet His enemy in the strength and guidance of the Holy Spirit.

The account of the Temptation is of peculiar value to us, for it represents an *autobiographical* segment of the Gospel records. Only Jesus and the devil were there to know all that happened in the wilderness. The devil was defeated; obviously he would not report the incident! And therefore "it is obvious that the substance of the narrative could have had only one source. No one has succeeded in suggesting any possible alternative."[2] There is neither Old Testament parallel, Messianic prophecy, nor Jewish or Christian legend

---

1. Op. cit., p. 83.
2. Alfred Plummer, *A Critical and Exegetical Commentary on the Gospel According to St. Luke,* The International Critical Commentary (Edinburgh: T. & T. Clark, 1910), p. 106.

that could have supplied the raw materials from which a Gospel writer could concoct such a story. Plummer correctly assesses the source: "It is from Christ Himself that the narrative comes; and He probably gave it to the disciples in much the same form as that in which we have it here."[3] Here then, from the Lord himself, is an account of how His holiness was assaulted and preserved.

In examining the record, the impression grows that our Lord understood himself, in the Temptation, to be God's true Israel, the faithful Remnant now reduced to the Servant-Son. The temptations should be viewed in comparison with those of Israel in the wilderness. It is noteworthy that Jesus overcame the temptations by quoting and applying passages from the Old Testament which are found in the record of Israel's testing and failure in the wilderness. Israel had been called out of Egypt to be the Son of God (cf. Exod. 4:22; Hos. 11:1). Thus Israel was a "holy" nation, standing in a unique relationship to God (Deut. 7:6). As such she had a mission to the world; she was to be an instrument of God for the world's redemption (Isa. 49:6).

Further, holiness for Israel meant a life of high ethical quality, as even a casual glance at the "Holiness Code" indicates (Lev. 19:1-17). But Israel, when tested, failed God and disqualified herself. Now "in Jesus, the wholly obedient Son of God, was to be seen in perfection all that Israel . . . had been intended to be, but through disobedience had never been."[4] Jesus, the true Israel, is triumphant in temptation, where the old Israel had suffered defeat.

With these preliminary observations made, we are now ready to view the temptation of Jesus as an attack upon His holiness.

---

3. Ibid.
4. Tasker, op. cit., p. 52.

1. *Jesus was tempted at the point of His unique relationship to God*

The tempter's first two assaults were prefaced with the words, "If You are the Son of God" (Matt. 4:3, 6). Whether or not Satan personally believed that Jesus was the Son of God, we cannot know. As Plummer comments, "The 'if' does not necessarily imply any doubt in Satan, although Augustine takes it so; but it is perhaps meant to inspire doubt in Jesus."[5]

The Father had just affirmed, "Thou art My Son." Now the devil counters the divine affirmation with an insinuation of doubt. Is it reasonable for the Son of God, that God to whom all the earth belongs, to endure the pangs of hunger? Is it not the privilege of the Son to participate freely in the fullness of the Father's bounties? The appeal to make bread out of stones is an appeal to "make use of the privileges of Sonship for violating its responsibilities."[6] But where Satan speaks of the Son's *rights*, Jesus answers in terms of *responsibility:* "It is written, 'MAN SHALL NOT LIVE ON BREAD ALONE, BUT ON EVERY WORD THAT PROCEEDS OUT OF THE MOUTH OF GOD'" (Matt. 4:4). Like all other men, He owes complete and joyful obedience to the will of God. Such obedience is the evidence of genuine sonship!

The second temptation takes note of this resolution of Jesus to live, at all cost, in the will of the Father, and to interpret that will from Scripture. Satan buttresses the challenge, "Throw Yourself down," by quoting a promise of divine protection imbedded in an ancient psalm. But that promise is not unconditional. Sonship means obedient trust; this is the form that sonship to God takes. To create deliberately a situation that puts God to the test is neither obedient

---

5. Op. cit., p. 109.
6. Morgan, op. cit., p. 168.

nor trustful. Rather, it is rebellion and disbelief that would invalidate the promise. "If He stepped out of the divine will He could no longer claim the divine care."[7] Jesus counters this misapplication and perversion of sonship with another passage from Holy Writ: "Again it is written, 'YOU SHALL NOT PUT THE LORD YOUR GOD TO THE TEST.'"

Thus did Satan launch an attack upon the uniqueness of Jesus—upon His sonship to God. He does not make outright denial of that sonship. He seeks to ruin it by reinterpreting sonship in a way that destroys its very essence, namely, unqualified acceptance of and acquiescence in the will of God the Father.

2. Jesus was tempted at the point of His redemptive involvement with men

As the Son, who was also the Servant, He came to deliver His people from their sins by taking those sins upon himself (cf. Isa. 53:6), that is, by substitutionary suffering. Satan desperately attempts, therefore, to defeat this element in Jesus' holiness by suggesting that He can accomplish the goal of redemption without suffering.

Thus, in the first assault he says, in effect, "With power to save others, surely You need not suffer hunger and deprivation. Why suffer when You can turn stones to bread!" "At the bottom," says A. B. Bruce, "the issue raised was selfishness or self-sacrifice."[8]

In the third temptation, Satan says, in effect, "Why suffer rejection and loneliness, when there is a way to possess the kingdoms of the earth that bypasses the Cross and the grave?" The temptation is that of "gaining power by compromise with evil. The danger is greatest when the end is

---

7. Ralph Earle, *Beacon Bible Commentary*, "Matthew," 6:58.
8. *The Synoptic Gospels*, in *The Expositor's Greek Testament* (New York: Geo. H. Doran Co., n.d.), 1:89.

good."[9] Satan is suggesting that "the end sanctifies the means." But Satan perverts the goal as well as the way to the goal. True, the Messiah Jesus was promised the kingdoms of the earth (Ps. 2:6-8). But as the Servant, He is to be the Salvation of the nations (Isa. 42:1-4), not just ruling over them but recreating them in justice. He is to reign in *righteousness*, not merely in power, turning men from the darkness and bondage of evil (Isa. 42:6-7). He cannot do this as a military Messiah such as popular Jewish thinking envisioned. He can do this only along the route of vicarious suffering at the hands of His own people (Isa. 53:10-11). Therefore, "He rejects the Jewish idea of the Messiah as an earthly potentate, and thus condemns Himself to rejection by His own people. . . . The end does not sanctify the means."[10]

Satan sought to destroy the qualifications of Jesus to be our Redeemer by dangling before Him the prospect of a conquest without a cross.

3. Jesus was tempted at the point of His moral perfection

The effort of Satan to inject doubt, and his attempt to confuse the Messianic portrait, had a single underlying purpose—to involve the holy Jesus in sin. Jesus came, not to smash His foes and rule as another Alexander or Caesar, but to redeem men from sin. To trap Him into sinning would disqualify Him for that mission, making Him a part of the illness instead of its cure. Thus, He is confronted by all the concentrated energy and cunning of the devil, who seeks to deceive and persuade Him into questioning the will of God, presuming upon the Word of God, and compromising the work of God. Over physical, spiritual, and vocational high-

9. Ibid., pp. 90-91.

10. Plummer, op. cit., p. 112.

ways[11] Satan travels in his malignant might to assault the holiness of Jesus, hoping to wreck the saving purpose of God.

Every diabolical effort fails. Jesus keeps unstained the soul that will be made an offering for sin. His victory was not without struggle and pain, for He suffered in being tempted (Heb. 2:18). "The temptations of Jesus are to be taken at face value. They are not sham battles but real struggles."[12] Not without anguish and moral exertion was the tempter repelled, but he was repelled! The holy Son of God came through victorious and launched a ministry that would take Him unflinching through humiliation, suffering, and death to the Resurrection, the dawn-burst of the new age of the kingdom of God.

* * *

We take up now the question of what all this means for the preaching of holiness.

1. First of all, *we have once again the revelation of divine holiness in Jesus*, this time under siege by the very ultimate force of unholiness in the universe. The transcendent majesty of God is mirrored in the uniqueness of Jesus as the only Son, a relationship sustained without defect in spite of the insinuations of doubt and the demands for proof made by Satan. The redemptive mercy of God is revealed in the willingness of Jesus, as Man and for men, to undergo the temptations. It is further shown in His deliberate choice to be Messiah according to the way of suffering marked out in Scripture. And the moral perfection of God becomes in Jesus a tested and perfected morality, for it was subjected to the tempter's seductions and prevailed over them without

---

11. Morgan, *The Voice of the Devil* (New York: Fleming H. Revell Co., n.d.), pp. 32-33.
12. Stagg, op. cit., p. 96.

compromise or tarnish. He was "tempted in all things as *we are, yet* without sin" (Heb. 4:15). We proclaim the tempted Christ as the triumph of holiness over unholiness!

2. *The value of His temptation as a paradigm cannot be overstressed.* Ernst Lohmeyer well says that "the New Testament . . . saw the narrative of the temptation of Jesus by the devil as the greatest and most profound example of a temptation."[13]

Jesus met temptation as our Representative, as "the Second Man" and "the Last Adam." He stood in the wilderness as Head of the new race, the redeemed humanity. Therefore when Satan said, "If You are the Son of God," Jesus responded, *"Man* shall not live on bread alone." Jesus was "committed to living man's life and sharing his lot, despite his supernatural origin."[14] So committed, He repulsed Satan, not by means of supernatural power beyond our exercise, but by means of the written Word of God within our grasp. He shows us how to be triumphant in temptation, and shows us at the same time how important it is to know the Scriptures. How can we excuse any capitulation to Satan when the only thing that hinders our attention to Scripture is the lethargy of our own hearts?

3. *The experience of Jesus reminds us, also, that "the holiest and highest in life have the most temptations."*[15] There is no degree of moral purity or of dedication to God's will that can immunize us against temptation in this life. Indeed, the more Christlike we become, the profounder our temptations will be. Temptation does not require sin within man for its basis. The unfallen Adam and the sinless Jesus were tempted. "Our temptability is not our shame, but our

---

13. *"Our Father"* (New York: Harper & Row, 1965), p. 193.
14. Harrison, op. cit., p. 85.
15. John Wycliffe, cited by Simcox, op. cit., p. 31.

dignity as children of God."[16] The warfare of Satan is unrelenting upon the saints of God. If Jesus was not spared, neither will His followers be exempt from severe temptations.

4. *The pattern of the Spirit-filled life emerges in this event of testing.* The Spirit anoints, not as a spiritual or emotional luxury, but to equip for service to God. That service must be given at the risk and cost of suffering for the sake of others. Jesus was led from the baptismal waters, not to some tranquil retreat, but to an encounter with Satan! Triumphant here, He begins a ministry of love and power that addresses multiform human need (cf. Matt. 4:23). That same pattern obtains with the first disciples. Filled with the Spirit at Pentecost, they are at once caught up in a program of service and suffering (see Acts 2:4; 3:6-8; 5:40-42; etc.). The same pattern will be repeated today. Being a Spirit-filled Christian does not mean an easy way. The holy life combines hardship and happiness in a strange but satisfying blend!

B. Holiness Triumphant

> And Jesus returned to Galilee in the power of the Spirit; and news about Him spread through all the surrounding district.
> And He began teaching in their synagogues and was praised by all.
> And He came to Nazareth, where He had been brought up; and as was His custom, He entered the synagogue on the Sabbath, and stood up to read.
> And the book of the prophet Isaiah was handed to Him. And He opened the book, and found the place where it was written,

---

16. Ibid., p. 32.

"THE SPIRIT OF THE LORD IS UPON ME,
BECAUSE HE ANOINTED ME TO PREACH THE GOS-
PEL TO THE POOR.
HE HAS SENT ME TO PROCLAIM RELEASE TO THE
CAPTIVES,
AND RECOVERY OF SIGHT TO THE BLIND,
TO SET FREE THOSE WHO ARE DOWNTRODDEN,
TO PROCLAIM THE FAVORABLE YEAR OF THE
LORD."

And He closed the book, and gave it back to the attendant, and sat down; and the eyes of all in the synagogue were fixed upon Him.

And He began to say to them, "Today this Scripture has been fulfilled in your hearing."

And all were speaking well of Him, and wondering at the gracious words which were falling from His lips; and they were saying, "Is this not Joseph's son?" (Luke 4:14-22).

And just then there was in their synagogue a man with an unclean spirit; and he cried out,

saying, "What do we have to do with You, Jesus of Nazareth? Have You come to destroy us? I know who You are—the Holy One of God!"

And Jesus rebuked him, saying, "Be quiet, and come out of him!"

And throwing him into convulsions, the unclean spirit cried out with a loud voice, and came out of him.

And they were all amazed, so that they debated among themselves, saying, "What is this? A new teaching with authority! He commands even the unclean spirits, and they obey Him" (Mark 1:23-27).

PARALLEL: Luke 4:33-35

The holiness of God, revealed in Jesus Christ, was attested at His baptism in the Jordan and tested by His temptation in the wilderness. The Synoptic Gospels are occupied next with the early Galilean ministry of Jesus, which Luke introduces with these words: "And Jesus returned to Galilee in the power of the Spirit" (Luke 4:14). He was "full of the Holy Spirit" when He entered the wilderness of testing, and now "in the power of the Spirit" He preaches, teaches, and heals. "Spiritual power," comments A. B. Bruce, is "not weakened by temptation, but rather strengthened."[17]

The first effects of His teaching ministry are noted briefly: "He was praised by all." Plummer attributes this praise to "the *power* of His preaching, especially when contrasted with the lifeless repetitions and senseless trivialities of ordinary teachers."[18] This praise-eliciting power is patently the power of the Spirit. It cannot be explained in terms of religious genius, natural abilities, acquired skills, or even by our badly overworked phrase, "outstanding personality." The Spirit of the Holy One was working in and through the Man, Jesus Christ.

This is not only the apostolic assessment of the ministry of Jesus; it is the explanation for His words and deeds which He himself gave. In the synagogue at Nazareth, Jesus outlined His ministry by use of passages from Isaiah the prophet: ". . . to preach the gospel to the poor . . . to proclaim release to the captives, and recovery of sight to the blind, to set free those who are downtrodden, to proclaim the favorable year of the Lord." Now the passage begins with these words, "The Spirit of the Lord is upon me, because He anointed me . . ." In saying to His listeners, "Today this Scripture has been fulfilled in your hearing," He identified "the source of his strength and the nature of his work."[19] As Simon Peter was later to assert, "God anointed Him with the Holy Spirit and with power, and He went about doing good, and healing all who were oppressed by the devil" (Acts 10:38). This much is perfectly clear, then, that the

---

17. Op. cit., p. 488.
18. Op. cit., p. 118.
19. A. R. C. Leaney, *A Commentary on the Gospel According to St. Luke*, Harper's New Testament Commentaries (New York: Harper & Brothers, 1958), p. 119.

power by which Jesus exercised His exciting ministry was "the Holy Spirit."

We have noted earlier that "Spirit" is used by Old Testament writers to designate the power by which God acts at the point of man's need. And this power is exercised in consonance with God's character as the Holy One. Therefore we may view the preaching, teaching, healing ministry of the Lord Jesus as the *triumph of divine holiness* over demonic and human evils.

1. *The ministry of Jesus is the triumph of the transcendent majesty of God*

This transcendence, as we have noted, is reflected in the uniqueness of Jesus as the Son of God. When Jesus refers the words of Isaiah to himself—"The Spirit of the Lord is upon me, because He anointed me"—He is consciously recalling the descent of the Spirit as a dove at His baptism. It was then that the Father spoke from heaven saying, "Thou art My beloved Son." A. D. Lys writes, in an article on "Anointing," "He is not one anointed among others, but He is the Anointed One *par excellence:* 'the Christ, the Son of the living God.'"[20]

This triumphant uniqueness of Jesus receives unsolicited testimony from "the spirit of an unclean demon," who had possessed an unfortunate man encountered by Jesus in the synagogue at Capernaum. The demon exclaimed in a loud voice, "I know who You are—the Holy One of God!" Jesus is the "One," the unique. No other is related to God in the same way as He is. No other, therefore, is "the Holy" in the same sense as He.

And as "the Holy One," He has power to command and to exorcise the demon. He merely speaks, "Be quiet and

---

20. Lys, in *A Companion to the Bible,* p. 21.

come out of him," and the demon obeys. True, the demon is sullen and rebellious, and convulses the man in making his exit. "The malice of the demon made the healing of the man as painful as possible."[21] But whatever last spasm of pain the demon may inflict, he is powerless to prevent the healing. The demon must yield to the word of Jesus! Amazement seizes the crowd of onlookers at this display of power by Jesus. "No formula of exorcism, no elaborate ritual, no prayer, but only one clear, commanding word. What a masterful person Jesus must have been!"[22] Masterful indeed, for He was incarnate Holiness, "the Holy One of God," the beloved Son!

2. *The ministry of Jesus is the triumph of the immanent mercy of God*

We have seen, from the Old and the New Testaments, that God's holiness means not only transcendence but immanence, and this immanence is especially related to His saving acts on behalf of His people. His immanence is redeeming mercy. This incursion of God into history to accomplish a gracious and delivering purpose is beautifully revealed in the ministry of Jesus.

He was "anointed" of God, and "anointing always designates a person for a particular work in the service of God."[23] His particular work, as He summarized it in His synagogue address at Nazareth, was to bring the gospel to the poor, release to the captives, healing to the blind, and freedom to the oppressed. In the prophecy of Isaiah, to the extent that these words were addressed to Israel in exile, the application was quite literal. But in the mind of Luke there

---

21. Plummer, op. cit., p. 135.
22. Hunter, op. cit., p. 33.
23. Lys, op. cit., p. 20.

is a "translation of all the categories named . . . from the political realm to the spiritual realm. Legitimately, for that was involved in the declaration that the prophecy was fulfilled in Jesus."[24] He came as the revelation of God's concern to deliver men from the "binding, blinding, grinding" effects of sin. The Isaiah passage promised release from captivity and restoration to Jerusalem which would fill the Jews with a joy like that experienced by remitted debtors and slaves in the year of jubilee. "It is obvious that both figures, the return from exile and the release at the jubilee, admirably express Christ's work of redemption."[25]

Jesus, familiar as He was with the prophecy of Isaiah, knew full well that the anointed Servant could accomplish His task as Redeemer only by suffering for those whom He sought to redeem. He would be taken captive and cruelly oppressed. He would suffer the heartbreak of betrayal and desertion by His friends, and of rejection and death by His enemies. He would lose sight of the Father's face, crying in blind anguish as darkness engulfed the Cross, "My God, My God, why hast Thou forsaken Me?" The power of the Holy Spirit is not exercised in His ministry without exacting from Him a terrible price. The holiness that conquers sin is a suffering holiness!

The horrible suffering that He would undergo was suggested early in His ministry. There in Nazareth the people "wondered," but they were not converted. His words are described as "gracious," but they did not prove convincing. The hometown congregation, so far from confessing Him to be "the Son of God," scoffed at Him as "Joseph's son." They were "filled with rage" and tried to cast Him from a cliff to His death on jagged rocks below. Because His hour

24. A. B. Bruce, op. cit., p. 490.
25. Plummer, op. cit., p. 121.

was not yet come, He escaped out of their hands. But He knew, even as He escaped, that the time would come when He must die by the rage of evil men in order to save them from their evil. He was prepared to make this sacrifice, to take all the unholiness of man upon His holiness that He might deliver them out of the bondage and blindness and bring them to God. The extent to which redemptive involvement is an element in the divine holiness finds its perfect fulfillment in the healing and saving ministry of the anointed suffering Servant.

3. The ministry of Jesus is the triumph of the perfect morality of God

The holiness of God revealed in Jesus includes the element of uncompromising antagonism to all that is evil and impure. This hostility is not passive but aggressive and mighty. It is dramatically pointed up in the encounter of Jesus with the demoniac in the Capernaum synagogue.

Mark describes this poor man as "a man with an unclean spirit." The phrase in Greek is literally "in" an unclean spirit. The man was under the power of the demon to such an extent "that his personality was sunk for a time in that of the spirit." [26] He was so utterly one with the demon as to be a subhuman embodiment of complete moral uncleanness. And he was accosted by Jesus, who was so uniquely one with God as to be the human embodiment of perfect moral purity. And "in the unique holiness of Jesus the evil spirit felt an *essentially hostile power*" [27] (emphasis mine). Therefore he cried out, "What have we to do with You, Jesus of Nazareth? Have You come to destroy us? I know who You are—the Holy One of God" (Mark 1:24).

Plummer well says that "it was not in flattery that the

---

26. Brown, op. cit., p. 138.
27. Plummer, op. cit., p. 134.

evil spirit thus addressed Him, but in horror. From the Holy One he could expect nothing but destruction."[28] There can be no question of an eternal dualism between good and evil! The demon fears, not punishment merely, but destruction. One of these hostile powers must do the other to its death, and demons know who will ultimately and absolutely triumph. "There is a mortal antithesis between Holy Spirit and unclean spirit which the demons recognize."[29] Christ anticipates His eschatological triumph over evil, Satanic and human, by silencing and evicting the unclean spirit, thus healing the man.

The triumph of Jesus, the incarnate Holy One of Israel, which we have traced in these passages is, of course, repeatedly demonstrated in His preaching, teaching, and healing ministry, as the entire Gospel records indicate. His conflict with unholiness is climaxed at the Cross and decisively proclaimed by the Resurrection. God and not Satan, holiness and not evil, will write the concluding glorious chapter of human history!

* * *

The preaching values of these passages are indeed exciting! They may be outlined as follows:

1. *To preach Christ is to preach the conflict of holiness with unholiness, and the victory of that divine holiness over every contending force of evil.* The message is a positive and assuring one! We can stand dauntless in the face of today's terrible erosion of morals—the wholesale captivity of men to the forces of war and crime, dope and drink,

---

28. Ibid.

29. Otto Procksch, *Theological Dictionary of the New Testament*, ed. Gerhard Kittel, trans. and ed. Geoffrey W. Bromiley (Grand Rapids: Wm. B. Eerdmans Publishing Co., 1964), 1:101-2.

irrationality and atheism—and dare to affirm that holiness shall finally and forever prevail over the worst conditions inflicted upon the world by evil. For the Creator and Redeemer of the world, who has revealed himself in Jesus, is a God irreconcilably and irresistibly opposed to sin. Every exorcism and healing performed by His only Son, Jesus, is a signpost stabbed deep into the soil of this age to point us forward in quenchless hope to the eternal age of righteousness, peace, and joy that will fulfill His patient purposes for man and the world. The Cross is a shaft of holiness driven into the very heart of evil, smiting it with a mortal wound, so that all the present raging of men and demons against God can be interpreted as the convulsions of an expiring victim!

2. *The passages remind us, however, that until the Second Coming there will be this raging of demons and men against God.* The ultimate victory of Jesus is hidden from those who do not believe. World conditions will drive them to despair and make them more easily the prey of evil powers. Therefore the positive message we proclaim may meet with a negative response from many to whom we address it. This was true in the case of Jesus himself. At the synagogue in Nazareth, He spoke "gracious words" in the power of the Spirit. Plummer insists that the true meaning of the adjective is "winning" rather than "gracious." He goes on to remark that "the words so calculated to win did not win the congregation. They were 'fulfilled in their ears,' but not in their hearts."[30]

If the ministry of Jesus met with varied responses, ranging from angry denial to happy faith, so will ours. We must not betray the triumph of holiness by permitting ourselves to become paralyzed by discouragement when some refuse to believe and obey the gospel. Keep preaching Jesus, what-

---

30. Op. cit., p. 125.

ever response listeners make, for in this way we participate more fully in the victory of divine holiness! Demons know that they are doomed to destruction. Let us be as wise as serpents.

3. Since we are yet in a period when holiness clashes with unholiness, let these passages also teach us anew that *whatever measure of effectiveness and success our preaching has depends upon an anointing from God.* If the perfect Servant, the very Enfleshment of God's holiness, required the anointing of God with the Holy Spirit in order to accomplish His ministry, how much more do we! It was in the power of the Spirit that the apostles labored, and no lesser equipment can suffice for their successors.

When the lame beggar was healed at the gate of the Temple, the crowd stared in wonder at the human agents, Peter and John, who hastened to deny that any personal holiness or power brought about the healing. But that a power linked with holiness did cause the man to walk is implicit in their denial. It was the power "in the name of Jesus Christ," and exercised through them only as they were men filled with the Spirit of Christ. A similar anointing is available to us, and indispensable to the achievement of Kingdom work by us today. Confronting the demonic forces that threaten men's destruction, and preaching the gospel of Christ that promises men's salvation, our deepest need as message-bearers is to be filled with the Holy Spirit.

This being true, there is wisdom, and challenge, for us in Luke's account of the anointing of Jesus. He tells us that "Jesus also was baptized, and *while He was praying,* heaven was opened, and the Holy Spirit descended upon Him" (3:21-22, emphasis mine).

PART TWO:

HOLY PEOPLE

"You shall be holy."

IV

The Experience of Holiness

A. Calling

> Then Jesus said to His disciples, "If any one wishes to come after Me, let him deny himself, and take up his cross, and follow Me.
>
> "For whoever wishes to save his life shall lose it; but whoever loses his life for My sake shall find it.
>
> "For what will a man be profited, if he gains the whole world, and forfeits his soul? Or what will a man give in exchange for his soul?
>
> "For the Son of Man is going to come in the glory of His Father with His angels; and WILL THEN RECOMPENSE EVERY MAN ACCORDING TO HIS DEEDS" (Matt. 16:24-27).

PARALLELS: Mark 8:34-38; Luke 9:23-26

The call to follow Jesus, recorded in Matt. 16:24-27, is a call to holiness. It sets forth simply and bluntly what it means to be the holy people of God in this age. This understanding, that discipleship equals holiness, becomes apparent when the passage is viewed in context. Peter confesses the Messiahship of Jesus, and in response to his confession Jesus declares that He will build His Church impregnable against its strongest foes (vv. 13-20). Jesus then interprets His Messiahship in terms of suffering, predicting His death and resurrection (v. 21). Peter reacts to this in stunned disbelief, and Jesus goes on to assert the necessity of cross-bearing for all who would be His disciples (vv. 22-27).

In these passages a complex of ideas emerges, all rooted in the Old Testament, which can be summarized in these propositions: (1) The Church is the new Israel, the community of the faithful which is gathered by the Messiah. (2) The Messiah reconstitutes Israel as His Church by virtue of His death and resurrection. He is thus the holy Lord of the Church, to whom His disciples stand related as His holy people. (3) The holiness of the Church, the new Israel, takes the form of radical obedience to the Lordship of Jesus.

Let us give closer attention to these propositions in order that we may see how the call to discipleship is a call to holiness.

1. *The Church is the new Israel, the holy nation of Messiah's present reign*

At Caesarea Philippi, Jesus raised the question, "Who do you say that I am?" Prompted by a divinely given insight, Peter responded, "Thou art the Christ, the Son of the living God." The reply of Jesus to this confession of faith was, "You are Peter, and upon this rock I will build My church, and the gates of Hades shall not overpower it."

This is the first of two instances, both of them occurring in Matthew, where Jesus calls His followers "the church." To penetrate His meaning we must remember that "the word *church* has deep roots in its O. T. use to designate the congregation of Israel."[1] Jesus obviously thinks of His Church, in its inception, as "a congregation within Israel which represents what all Israel should be and seeks to win all Israel."[2] The Church is the congregation that He gathers, the community that He establishes, as the Messiah. In contrast to "all Israel," the national Israel, His people are "a congregation within" the nation, the spiritual Israel.

The Messiah's forerunner, John the Baptist, had foretold this separation and selection. According to John, Messiah would separate the wheat from the chaff, garnering the former into the granary of His kingdom, and destroying the latter with fire. The basis of this separation would be, not physical descent from Abraham, but repentance and faith in this Coming One (Matt. 3:7-12). John's prophetic warnings and promises were in substantial agreement with the Messianic hope aroused by the Old Testament and kept aflame in the best thought of Judaism. It was believed that the new-age Redeemer would "fulfill his mission by grouping around him the community of the true faithful, distinct from the nation."[3]

We recognize this idea of a faithful minority within the nation of Israel as the Old Testament doctrine of the remnant. Paul's insight, that "they are not all Israel who are descended from Israel" (Rom. 9:6), stems from the psalmists and prophets of the Old Testament (cf. 1 Kings 19:18; Ps. 50:5; Isa. 1:9; 10:20 ff.; Amos 5:15). "Within the empirical covenant community of Israel" was "a smaller group, who were in practice what the whole community was in theory.

---

1. Filson, op. cit., p. 187.
2. Ibid.
3. Menoud, op. cit., p. 51.

. . . This inner group of faithful souls is sometimes designated as a 'remnant.'"[4] The remnant took covenant obligations seriously and tried to carry them out. However apostate the nation at large became, a remnant was loyal to Yahweh, and accordingly a remnant was spared from otherwise complete destruction and abandonment of the nation (cf. Rom. 9:27-29). It was this remnant which made possible "the fulfillment of God's promises to Israel. So long as there was a recognizable Israel, however small, in which these promises could be realized, there was no fear that they should come to nothing."[5]

Jesus came as the anointed Servant, the promised Messiah, to gather this remnant and thus reconstitute the congregation of Israel. From the nation at large, blind apostates following blind leaders, "He separated a small company which stood in sharp contrast to Pharisaic scribes and ultimately to the whole stiffnecked people."[6] This small company "represented the true people of God, i.e., the church."[7] This, then, was the situation at Caesarea Philippi. The disciples confessed that Jesus was the Messiah, the Son and Servant of that God who is "living," that is, who is active in the affairs of history to save a people for himself. And Jesus said, in effect, "Yes, I am the Messiah, and you are the Messianic community, the new Israel." As Bruce points out, the very number of His inner circle of followers, the chosen *Twelve*, "implied that they represented the faithful remnant of the Old Israel who would also be the foundation of the new."[8]

---

4. F. F. Bruce, *The New Testament Development of Old Testament Themes* (Grand Rapids: Wm. B. Eerdmans Publishing Co., 1968), p. 57.

5. Ibid., p. 59.

6. K. L. Schmidt, *Theological Dictionary of the New Testament*, 3:520-21.

7. Ibid.

8. F. F. Bruce, *The NT Development*, p. 62.

2. The Church, as the new people of God, is established by the death and resurrection of Jesus, the Messiah

When the dual identification is made, Jesus as the Messiah and the disciples as the Church, our Lord proceeds to make His first unambiguous prediction of His suffering, death, and resurrection. "From that time Jesus Christ began to show His disciples that He must go to Jerusalem, and suffer many things from the elders and chief priests and scribes, and be killed, and be raised up on the third day."

Peter's confession forms the "hinge" of each Synoptic Gospel. G. E. P. Cox describes the confession of Peter as "the psychological moment" for initiating the disciples into "the inmost secret" of Messiahship, that "by an awful paradox the Messiah must die, formally rejected by the leaders of God's chosen people." This *must* is "a moral necessity imposed by the exigencies of human blindness and sin."[9] Nonetheless, it is ordained by God and will be vindicated by the resurrection of the slain Messiah.

Alas, the disciples shared so fully in this "human blindness and sin" that they rejected with horror the idea of a suffering Messiah. Jesus had used the title "Son of Man," which in popular Messianic expectation had been associated with a heavenly Conqueror, not a passive Sufferer. To the measure in which they shared the distorted hope, the disciples were not able, as Jesus was, to synthesize this Ruler of Daniel's vision with the Sufferer of Isaiah's prophecy. Consequently, Peter mars his great confession by flinging the Passion prediction from him in dismay: "God forbid it, Lord! This shall never happen to You!" (Matt. 16-22). He thus won for himself a withering rebuke, for Jesus recog-

---

9. *The Gospel According to St. Matthew*, Torch Bible Commentaries (London: SCM Press, 1952), p. 113.

nized in Peter's protest a repetition of Satan's strategy of temptation—"a whisper from hell to move him from his purpose to suffer."[10] Once again the tempter was saying, "Gain Your kingdom in some way that avoids the Cross." But "the earthly mission of Jesus, and still more His death and resurrection, have as their aim the formation of a community of the faithful."[11] To reach that goal He must travel the divinely appointed route, the Via Dolorosa. Apart from the bloody Cross and empty grave He cannot be the true Messiah and cannot gather them as the true Israel.

Israel was a *covenant* community. God chose Israel to be His own possession, the holy nation of the holy God, by redeeming them from Egypt and establishing a covenant with them at Sinai (cf. Deut. 7:6-11). The death of Jesus is to be the means of establishing the new covenant promised to the remnant (cf. Jer. 31:31-34; Matt. 26:26-28). The new covenant community, the Church, owes its very existence to the Passion which Peter so vehemently opposed!

Israel, as God's people of the covenant, was to be holy. "You shall be holy; for I the Lord your God am holy" (Lev. 19:2). Their holiness was to assume the form of obedience to covenant stipulations imposed by the will of God. Thus the ethical injunctions of the "Holiness Code" are given force by the reiterated statement, "I am the Lord" (Leviticus 19). And now it is plain why the call to discipleship is a call to holiness. As Jesus could not be the Messiah except in obedience to the will of the Father, which meant the pathway of suffering, so the disciples cannot be the people of God, the new Israel, the holy nation, except in obedience to the Messiah's will. And this also means following Him along the way of suffering. Thus He says, "If anyone wishes to

---

10. Brown, op. cit., p. 89.
11. Menoud, op. cit., p. 52.

come after Me, let him deny himself, and take up his cross, and follow Me."

3. The holiness of the Church, the new Israel, must take the form of radical obedience to the Lord Jesus Christ

Followers of the Messiah must embrace a way of life "which banishes selfish concern and is ready for self-sacrifice even to death."[12] Our relationship to Him is a covenant relationship, and these are His covenant stipulations. In accepting or rejecting them, we accept or reject Him as our holy Lord, and we accept or reject ourselves as His holy people. What is at stake in the decision He compels us to make is nothing more nor less than our very existence, our lives. In the words of Dietrich Bonhoeffer, "Just as Christ is Christ only in virtue of his suffering and rejection, so the disciple is a disciple only in so far as he shares his Lord's suffering and rejection and crucifixion. Discipleship means adherence to the person of Jesus, and therefore submission to the law of Christ which is the law of the cross."[13]

The condition of discipleship becomes the expression of new covenant holiness. That condition is self-denial and cross-bearing.

Denial of self "is far more radical than denying something to oneself. . . . He meant a yes to God and no to oneself."[14] What saying no to oneself involves is the courageous refusal to save or protect oneself by dodging the cross. As Tasker puts it, "It means saying 'No' to the imperious sinful ego, which not only puts self first, but makes 'safety first' its primary aim."[15]

---

12. Filson, op. cit., p. 189.
13. *The Cost of Discipleship* (New York: Macmillan Co., 1949), p. 77.
14. Stagg, op. cit., p. 176.
15. Op. cit., p. 61.

The reference of Jesus to a cross must not be watered down or sentimentalized. Those to whom He spoke were grimly familiar with crosses. In Galilee, hundreds of brave but foolish followers of self-appointed messiahs had been crucified by the Romans. The cross represented "not so much a burden as an instrument of death."[16] The cross was to die upon, and His followers are called to consign their selves, their own wills, to death.

To take up one's cross means "death to self . . . a full surrender of one's will to God's will."[17] God's will means life, to be sure, but it is resurrection life. It lies beyond death, beyond the execution of everything rebellious and traitorous within us that would oppose His will to spare ourselves from suffering (Gal. 2:20). "When Christ calls a man," wrote Bonhoeffer, "he bids him come and die. . . . Only the man who is dead to his own will can follow Christ."[18]

This passage may be regarded as a ledger of decision. On the one side we are to reckon the cost of following Jesus. It is death to self-centeredness and consent to trials, suffering, even martyrdom. On the other hand we are to compute the cost of not following Him. We may, by sparing ourselves from His rule, gain the world. But the cost of such selfish existence will be the loss of our souls, so that any real profit is impossible. Between these options, therefore, we must decide, weighing the decision in the light of coming judgment (v. 27).

"To sacrifice permanent spiritual welfare for temporary physical safety or comfort is a bad bargain."[19] The bargain is bad because the answer to Jesus' question, "What will a man give in exchange for his soul?" can only be, "Nothing of equal or comparable value!" "The soul, the spiritual life, is

---

16. Plummer, op. cit., p. 248.
17. Ralph Earle, op. cit., p. 158.
18. Op. cit., p. 79.
19. Filson, op. cit., p. 189.

64

incommensurable with any outward possession however great, and if forfeited the loss is irrevocable."[20]

"The Son of Man is going to come in the glory of His Father with His angels; and WILL THEN RECOMPENSE EVERY MAN ACCORDING TO HIS DEEDS." The Son of Man must suffer, but humiliation and suffering are only part of the story. The Son of Man will come in glory as the Judge of us all. How tragic to reject the present cross and miss the future glory! How utter and unrelieved the folly of pampering and protecting the self, dodging the cross of discipleship, only to face that judgment and discover that the loss of life has crystallized into permanence!

"Follow Me," says Jesus. And in these words He sets the holy life of the new covenant before us in the familiar figure of a journey to be made. Godet quaintly comments: "The man who has made up his mind to set out on a journey, has first of all to say farewell; here he has to bid adieu to his own life, to deny himself. Next there is luggage to carry; in this case it is the cross, the sufferings and reproach which never fail to fall on him who pays a serious regard to holiness of life."[21]

"You shall be holy to me;" said God to ancient Israel, "for I the Lord am holy, and have separated you from the peoples, that you should be mine" (Lev. 20:26). Holiness means "exclusively the Lord's." "Follow Me," says Jesus. Be exclusively Mine. Live under My Lordship. Tolerate no rival claims upon your allegiance, whether made by others, by the world, or by your own will. Deny yourself. Put self-interest to its death and steadfastly follow Me! When the early Christians confessed, "Jesus is Lord," as their initial creed, and when at the peril of martyrdom they refused to

---

20. A. B. Bruce, op. cit., p. 227.

21. *Commentary on the Gospel of Luke*, Classic Commentary Library (reprint ed., Grand Rapids: Zondervan Publishing House, n.d.), p. 418.

acknowledge the lordship of the emperor as absolute, they were living as the new Israel, the holy nation, God's own people! The call to discipleship is a call to holiness.

* * *

What are we to make of this in our holiness preaching?

1. *The roots of our message must be biblical, grounded in the Old and New Testaments, not in the theology, psychology, or sociology of any period of history.* We need to recall, therefore, that holiness is a *relational* term primarily, and not an ethical one. It marks someone or something as the exclusive property of God, separated for and devoted to Him who is "the Holy One." Therefore the experience and life of holiness *begins* with the summons to follow Jesus, and not with a "second" or "deeper" experience, although it goes on through these. To follow Him is to follow the Messiah, who is the Revelation of "the Holy One of Israel," and thus to live as a member of His new Israel, the holy people of God.

2. The equation of discipleship and holiness preserves another scriptural truth, namely, that *the ethic of holiness is fundamentally a faith-obedience ethic.* True, it is also a love ethic, and we rightly make much of this. But the love ethic itself is based upon the faith-obedience ethic. Our love is commanded in Scripture! G. Campbell Morgan spoke of holiness as "love-mastered life." It is truer to say that holiness is "Christ-mastered life." Love is not an abstraction that can somehow be substituted for personal obedience to His Lordship. Holiness is discipleship, living under the rule of Christ, wherever that leads and whatever that costs!

3. *"Following Jesus" is the positive expression of holiness which has as its negative condition the crucifixion of self.* There must be, in the Christian's life, some very real counterpart to Gethsemane where, by resolutely submitting

66

his will to the will of God, he consents to the cross that slays self-centeredness. Because the Cross has become such a valued symbol for Christ's redeeming work, we find it difficult to realize how Jesus' words about cross-bearing jarred the disciples. "It requires real historical imagination to feel the sinister ring of these words as the disciples must have heard them. 'If you want to be my disciples,' Jesus says in effect, 'you must begin to live as men on their way to a gallows.' "[22]

In our affluent times, in the midst of our treasure-leisure-pleasure-oriented culture, the gallows experience is hard to accept. "Dying out" is an expression we seldom hear in our churches these days! But living crucified is still the only legitimate discipleship. We must, as those who by preaching stand in Christ's stead, call our people to die in order to live!

4. *Discipleship to Jesus, as New Testament holiness, gives a broad scope to our preaching.* Every related text in the Gospels, where He issues the call and states the cost of discipleship, is a vital point in the full circle of holiness preaching. One has but casually to read the Gospels to see how numerous such passages are. We have more than one or two strings to fiddle on! There can be no excuse for "sameness, lameness, and tameness" in our ministry of proclaiming holiness.

B. Cleansing

> But when he saw many of the Pharisees and Sadducees coming for baptism, he said to them, "You brood of vipers, who warned you to flee from the wrath to come?
>
> "Therefore bring forth fruit in keeping with repentance;

---

22. Hunter, op. cit., p. 90.

and do not suppose that you can say to yourselves, 'We have Abraham for our father'; for I say to
you, that God is able from these stones to raise up
children to Abraham.

"And the axe is already laid at the root of the
trees; every tree therefore that does not bear good
fruit is cut down and thrown into the fire.

"As for me, I baptize you with water for repentance, but He who is coming after me is mightier
than I, and I am not fit to remove His sandals; He himself will baptize you with the Holy Spirit and fire.

"And His winnowing fork is in His hand, and He
will thoroughly clear His threshing floor; and He will
gather His wheat into the barn, but He will burn up
the chaff with unquenchable fire" (Matt. 3:7-12).

PARALLELS: Mark 1:4-8; Luke 3:7-17

The holiness of the Church and the individual Christian
arises from two sources: (1) The relationship to Jesus Christ,
who, as we have seen, is the Holy Offspring in whom the
holiness of God is revealed. Called into His fellowship and
living under His Lordship, the Church is holy, the Christian
is holy. (2) The reception of the Holy Spirit, who, by infilling the hearts of believers, effects within them a profound moral cleansing. This second source depends upon
the first, for "the Holy Spirit's coming upon Jesus in
fulness also qualified Him to bestow the Holy Spirit upon
His disciples."[23] The preaching of John reached its zenith in
his prediction that the Messiah would baptize with the Holy
Spirit. This prediction is the subject of our present investi-
gation.

Matthew 3:11-12 and its parallels are appropriately
captioned "John's Messianic Preaching" in Huck's famous
Synopsis. It is concerned with the ministry of the Messiah
who was so eagerly awaited by Israel. Luke informs us that

---

23. E. Y. Mullins, "The Holy Spirit," The International Standard
Bible Encyclopaedia, 3:1411.

the people were "in a state of expectation and . . . wondering in their hearts about John, as to whether he might be the Christ" (Luke 3:15). In reply to their queries, John spoke the words we are now considering. In the account by Matthew a Messianic title is preserved—"He who is coming," or "The Coming One." Schneider calls this a "traditional Messianic title," and says that "in the Messianic dogma of Judaism the Messiah is the coming One . . . who with His coming inaugurates the time of salvation."[24] While some deny that "the Coming One" was a common Messianic title,[25] few would dispute Tasker's mediating position that it was "virtually, though not technically, a title for the Messiah, owing to the frequent references in the Old Testament to His coming."[26]

John was not the Messiah. As a "voice in the wilderness," he could proclaim the imminent arrival of "the kingdom of heaven." And he could baptize in water a sins-confessing people who would become Messiah's community. But the judging and saving work associated with the Kingdom was far beyond John's power. He could not do that work; he could only summon the people to repent and believe on the Coming One. The Coming One was mightier; He could produce the reality of which John's baptism was but the symbol. The Messiah could and would baptize "with the Holy Spirit and fire."

In John's Messianic preaching the accent is on judgment. The One who comes will bring "the wrath to come" (v. 7). According to popular belief among the Jews, the Messiah was to administer God's cleansing judgment. Popular theory reserved this judgment for the Gentiles. But with a courage reminiscent of Amos, John dares to relate it to "the

---

24. *Theological Dictionary of the New Testament*, 2:670-72.
25. For example, Filson, op. cit., p. 136.
26. Op. cit., p. 118.

people," that is, to Israel. Even the leaders of the chosen nation, "the Pharisees and Sadducees" (v. 7), were not exempt.

This judgment would begin by taking the form of a radical separation. Within the nation as it was then constituted, a new nation would emerge, a true Israel determined, not by physical descent from Abraham, but by penitence and faith (vv. 8-9). Upon this new Israel the Messiah would pour out the Holy Spirit, the promised Gift of the new age (see Ezek. 36:25-27; Joel 2:28 ff.). The effect of the baptism with the Spirit would be life and cleansing, so suitably symbolized by the water baptism which John administered. Those who did not repent, who rejected the sign of John's baptism in water, made up a false Israel whose end was to be destruction—the "unquenchable fire." The distinct groups within the nation as a whole are described under the contrasting figures of fruitful and unfruitful trees, and wheat and chaff.

Because Messiah's work of judgment is set forth under the figure of *fire* in verses 10 and 12, many commentators from Origen onward have linked the phrase "and fire" in verse 11 to this judgment also. The word "fire" is given the same significance in all three verses, so that *two baptisms* are predicted in verse 11, one life-giving and purifying, the other death-dealing and punishing. John's preaching, thus viewed, sets before Israel the decision of holiness or hell. In this vein Filson writes, "The Stronger One will execute a double ministry. To those who respond in repentance . . . he will give the Holy Spirit. . . . But to those who do not repent he will bring the fire of judgment." [27] He is convinced that "fire" in verse 11 cannot mean the Holy Spirit's "kindly presence and power," since verse 12 obviously refers to the flames of divine judgment.

---

27. Op cit., p. 66. Also, Stagg, op. cit.; A. B. Bruce, op. cit.

On the other hand, a line of learned and devout commentators stretching back to Chrysostom regards "and fire" as epexegetical; that is, the phrase expands and explains the preceding words, "with the Holy Spirit." In this case "fire" points to the fiery character of the Spirit's sanctifying ministry in the lives of the people of the Messiah. Frequent reference is made by these scholars to the visible symbol of fire at Pentecost (Acts 2:3), and frequent allusion is made to Malachi's prediction of the Messianic ministry as "a refiner's fire," which will "purify the sons of Levi and refine them like gold and silver" (Mal. 3:2-3). David Brown writes, "Clearly . . . it is but the fiery character of the Spirit's operations upon the soul—searching, consuming, refining, sublimating."[28] Similarly Calvin says, "The word 'fire' is added as an epithet, and is applied to the Spirit, because he takes away our pollutions, as fire purifies gold."[29]

The evidence seems to support those who interpret "fire" to mean a penal alternative to the baptism with the Holy Spirit. This interpretation is more consistent with the context. "Fire" in verses 10 and 12 controls the reference in verse 11.

John's message was *spoken and heard*, and this denies to men the leisurely distinctions permitted by examination of a written text. When he had just mentioned fire in a judgment sense, and would immediately go on to speak of fire again in a judgment sense, could his listeners have understood the middle statement to mean fire in a remedial and purgative sense? *Listening* to John, as he speaks of contrasting groups and destinies, the three allusions to fire in the three successive statements, of which judgment is a

28. Op. cit., p. 12.
29. John Calvin, *Commentary on a Harmony of the Evangelists* (Grand Rapids: Wm. B. Eerdmans Publishing Co., 1949), p. 190. Also, Henry Alford, *The Greek Testament* (London: Rivington's, 1859); Earle, op. cit.

dominant theme, would not be readily understood now as punishing, but now as purifying, and now again as punishing flames. Henry Cowles said long ago, "The general drift of thought in the passage ought to control the interpretation of this phrase; and this drift is plainly in the line of retribution."[30]

It further seems that Acts 1:5 is impressive, if not decisive, for the interpretation of Matt. 3:11. With the new Israel before Him, the penitent and believing disciples not now mixed with unbelievers, the risen Lord repeated the promise of baptism with the Spirit. And although the contrast with John's water baptism is preserved, the mention of "fire" is now omitted!

Be that as it may, whatever the reading of the text, an experience of inward cleansing is certainly implied. The *Holy* Spirit bears well His name, for He not only *is* holy, but He *makes* holy. The testimony of Simon Peter recorded in Acts 15:8-9 captures the essence of the baptism with the Spirit in its effects. He makes no mention of the inaugural signs that accompanied the Spirit's coming at Pentecost—the wind and fire and tongues. Rather, the abiding significance of the Pentecostal baptism occupies him, and so he declares: "'God, who knows the heart, bore witness to them, giving them the Holy Spirit, just as He also did to us . . . *cleansing their hearts by faith*'" (emphasis mine).

The promise in Matt. 3:11 was fulfilled at Pentecost. Now this question must be raised: Is the baptism with the Holy Spirit a valid promise to believers today? Some sincere and serious students of Scripture say no, and point to the absence of any command or promise to be "baptized" with the Spirit after the event at Pentecost. This is quite true. However, to those who were already Christians, Paul writes, "Be filled with the Spirit" (Eph. 5:18). If there is no in-

---

30. *Matthew and Mark* (New York: D. Appleton & Co., 1891), p. 23.

junction to be baptized with the Spirit, there is plainly an injunction to be "filled." "Filled" is the very term used to describe the result of the outpouring of the Spirit upon the disciples in the Upper Room: "They were all filled with the Holy Spirit." Surely the inner results of being "filled" today will be just what they were then—a cleansing of the heart from sin, with the Spirit indwelling a purified residence and empowering the witness of believers.

The Coming One has come. By His life, death, and resurrection Jesus, the Messiah, has inaugurated the new age. Through the gospel He is gathering His true Israel. To those who repent and believe, the new-age Gift—the Holy Spirit in life-giving, sin-purging, mission-energizing fullness—is promised. This is the message of full salvation that is to be borne joyfully to our day. The historical fact yields to the existential decision! Has the Coming One come to our hearts? Has He filled us with the cleansing Holy Spirit? The strategic moment, when we are confronted with this word of Scripture, is crowded with eschatological urgency, for the "fire" is still the terrible alternative, and "the wrath to come" is drawing closer.

* * *

The preaching values of the passage with respect to holiness now claim our attention.

1. *The Church, in its visible and statistical aspects, represents today a situation comparable to that within national Israel at the time of the Baptist's preaching.* Many within the nation were not Israelites in truth. Despite their facade of religion, rituals, and respectability, their hearts were in revolt against God and their lives were immersed in sin. And within the Church today there are multitudes for whom Christianity is but a form, a creed, a veneer of religious culture overlaying lives that contradict everything that Jesus came to do. The Coming One, at His second

coming, will surely separate the true from the false. Trumpet voices with prophetic courage are needed to call a compromised and complacent Christendom to repentance and holiness.

2. *Those who strive earnestly to be Christ's followers need an inward cleansing and power equal to, and greater than, the pressures against them,* as they live in the midst of a godless age, and a worldly Church. This needed cleansing and power are available in, and only in, the experience of being filled with the Spirit. The Messiah has an inner lustration to bestow wherever His promise is grasped with faith. We need to preach positively and persistently the possibility of being holy people, not only because we belong to the holy Lord, but also because the Holy Spirit resides in us and presides over us as a mighty Cleanser.

3. Now, as then, *the alternative to the life of the Spirit is the fire of judgment.* The destruction of chaff is as surely the Messiah's responsibility as is the conservation of wheat. He has pledged to return and recompense every man according to his doings. Doing hinges upon being, and being wholeheartedly Christian demands hearts that are purified and sustained in purity by the abiding presence of the Holy Spirit. The truth of the judgment to come is a missing note in much of today's preaching. More hard-hitting, biblical messages that remind men of their appointment with God to give an account of their lives would go far to increase the number within the Church who recognize the importance of being filled with the Spirit.

C. Continuation

"Then the kingdom of heaven will be comparable to ten virgins, who took their lamps, and went out to meet the bridegroom.
"And five of them were foolish, and five were prudent.

74

"For when the foolish took their lamps, they took no oil with them,

but the prudent took oil in flasks along with their lamps.

"Now while the bridegroom was delaying, they all got drowsy and began to sleep.

"But at midnight there was a shout, 'Behold, the bridegroom! Come out to meet him.'

"Then all those virgins arose, and trimmed their lamps.

"And the foolish said to the prudent, 'Give us some of your oil, for our lamps are going out.'

"But the prudent answered, saying, 'No, there will not be enough for us and you too; go instead to the dealers and buy some for yourselves.'

"And while they were going away to make the purchase, the bridegroom came, and those who were ready went in with him to the wedding feast; and the door was shut.

"And later the other virgins also came, saying, 'Lord, Lord, open up for us.'

"But he answered and said, 'Truly I say to you, I do not know you.'

"Be on the alert then, for you do not know the day nor the hour" (Matt. 25:1-13).

And his father Zacharias was filled with the Holy Spirit, and prophesied, saying:

"Blessed be the Lord God of Israel,
For He has visited us and accomplished redemption
   for His people,
And has raised up a horn of salvation for us
In the house of David His servant—
As He spoke by the mouth of His holy prophets from
   of old—
Salvation FROM OUR ENEMIES,
And FROM THE HAND OF ALL WHO HATE US;
To show mercy toward our fathers,
And to remember His holy covenant,
The oath which He swore to Abraham our father,
To grant us that we being delivered from the hand of
   our enemies,
Might serve Him without fear,

In holiness and righteousness before Him all our days"
(Luke 1:67-75).

To have experienced cleansing from sin in the past is not enough! The believer is on a journey beset with trials and perils to its very end. No previous experience of grace can provide momentum sufficient for us to coast to heaven! We must renew daily our decision in faith to follow Christ and to be His holy people. The crisis of cleansing must be followed by the process of growth and maturation. Purity must be vigilantly maintained against every threat of evil. Not until we have reached the goal can there be utter relaxation. The past does not guarantee the future, and the past is always threatened by the present.

The hope of the Christian is focused upon the return of Jesus Christ. He plainly affirmed His coming again, and He warned His followers that the age between the advents would be one of tribulation. Therefore, He said, "the one who endures to the end, he shall be saved" (Mark 13:13).

But the threat to discipleship and holiness does not come always from the persecuting world. It arises out of the temptation to grow careless and negligent as the return of Christ seems to be delayed. This is the force of the parable of the 10 virgins, where the necessity of persevering in the Spirit-filled life is dramatically set forth. That lifelong holiness is possible is clearly stated in the Benedictus of Zacharias. These two passages will occupy our attention now. Our study must be not merely academic as we view them. Rather, the question of *our* continuation in holiness should exercise our minds, for we are pilgrims, not just students.

1. *Holiness must involve constant readiness for the coming of Jesus Christ*

That He is coming again is the unmistakable message of the New Testament. His return in glory to judge and reign over men is the blessed hope of the Church. No thoughtful Christian would exchange that future for any of the secular utopias being proposed by sociologists and theologians today.

That one may not be prepared for His coming, as the result of sheer carelessness, is the burden of the parable of the 10 virgins. "It is a warning against false security."[31] The thrust of the parable is simple to state and its urgency impossible to exaggerate—"Be prepared!"[32] The lost opportunity dramatized by the closed door stands as an awful reminder of the price one may pay for spiritual neglect!

The virgins who pled in vain through that closed door are not described as evil but as foolish. While the description of Simcox—"brainless beauties"[33]—seems gratuitous, we can certainly go along with the comment of A. B. Bruce that "even the 'foolish' might be very attractive, lovable girls."[34] One need not prove morally degenerate to miss the wedding feast, only spiritually careless!

We must not misunderstand the closing injunction to "watch." The warning is "not directed against sleep but against lack of foresight."[35] All the virgins slept, and in view of the excitement of the occasion and the lateness of the hour, their dozing is perfectly natural. The tragedy occurs when, awaking to greet the bridegroom, some discover that their lamps are going out. "If properly prepared, one may be at his normal work (xxiv. 40f), or sleeping, but one must have the resources with which to meet the Lord whenever his sudden coming occurs."[36]

---

31. Joachim Jeremias, *The Parables of Jesus* (New York: Charles Scribner's Sons, 1963), p. 175.

32. A. M. Hunter, *Interpreting the Parables* (Philadelphia: Westminster Press, 1960), p. 84.

33. Op. cit., p. 269.

34. Op. cit., p. 299.

35. Ibid., p. 301.

36. Filson, op. cit., p. 264.

Not only did they all sleep, but all alike expected the bridegroom to appear! The parable is not directed against persons who have abandoned or denied the hope of Christ's coming again. The folly of "the foolish virgins" was not their "want of expectation that the bridegroom would come . . . but their not having any provision for meeting him in case he should tarry."[37]

The preparation for His coming does not lie in the fact that one believes in that return doctrinally, but in the fact that one is spiritually ready at all times. The opportunity to get ready may be lost by the sudden appearing of our Lord. "There is a time for preparation and a time when it is too late to prepare. This is the point of emphasis."[38]

Obviously, the bridegroom in the story is Jesus himself. While H. L. Ellison pointedly warns that "the parable is refractory to any allegorical treatment" of its details,[39] he interprets it with reference to the coming of the Son of Man in judgment. There is no reason to question the judgment of the majority of commentators, of whom Cox is representative: "The bridegroom is the *divine* bridegroom of the O.T. (cf. Hos. 2:16; Isa. 59:6) identified in the N.T. with the Christ (II Cor. 11:2; Rev. 19:7)."[40] Just as many of the contemporaries of Jesus were not prepared at His first coming, "Matthew is warning the men of his day, even in the Church, that the same thing will happen at the Second."[41]

If Jesus is the bridegroom, what is the oil that feeds the lamps, and stands as the symbol of readiness? Here the interpreters have asserted such a variety of opinions that the

---

37. Brown, op. cit., p. 117.

38. Stagg, op. cit., p. 223.

39. *A New Testament Commentary*, "The Gospel According to Matthew," ed. G. C. D. Howley (Grand Rapids: Zondervan Publishing House, 1969), p. 169.

40. Op. cit., p. 149.

41. Ibid.

caution of Ellison noted above is well taken. A. B. Bruce long ago complained that "every interpreter has his own conjecture. The oil is faith, charity, almsgiving, desire for the praise of God rather than the praise of men; good works in general, the Holy Spirit, diligence in the culture of grace, religious joy. In short, it is anything you please; each conjecture is purely arbitrary, one is as legitimate as another, and the multiplicity of opinions justifies the inference that they are all alike illegitimate."[42]

But is he right? There is one recurring interpretation that is not all that arbitrary, but has some warrant in the Scripture. Earle writes, "Since oil is a recognized type of the Holy Spirit, both in the Old Testament and the New, it is suggested that we must be filled with the Spirit if we would be properly prepared."[43] In similar vein Morgan says, "In the supply of the Spirit of God, and the life yielded to that Spirit, and dominated by that Spirit, there is always the oil which provides the light."[44] Indeed, the Holy Spirit, in His indwelling and purifying fullness, is the Source of those spiritual characteristics which Bruce cites from many exegetes. He is the Source of our joy, growth, good works, desire for God's praise, deeds of charity, and faith. He is the Life of God in the soul of man. He is the Force that inwardly conforms us to the likeness of Christ. He is the Illuminator of the sacred Word that nourishes our faith and hope in Christ's return. It is inconceivable that one could be always ready for that coming unless he was filled with and guided by the Spirit. And it is equally inconceivable that one so filled and led should not be prepared!

The refusal of the prudent virgins to share their oil has

---

42. *The Parabolic Teaching of Christ* (New York: A. C. Armstrong and Son, 1908), p. 502.

43. Op. cit., p. 225.

44. *The Parables and Metaphors of Our Lord* (New York: Fleming H. Revell Co., 1943), p. 151.

been interpreted by some scholars as churlish and selfish. But surely this is pressing the story too far, for it seems quite obvious that Jesus was, by the device of their reply, making a decisive point, namely, that "the grace of God is not transferable."[45] He is further warning that when He comes, "if the grace of Christian character is not by then a personal possession, it will be too late to acquire it."[46] If we would be ready to meet the Lord at His coming we must possess this grace of being indwelt by the sanctifying Spirit, and by this grace we must be sustained daily and hourly!

Those who are ready shall enter into the wedding banquet. The future of the saints is consistently portrayed in terms of joy, and joy associated with their intimate fellowship with Jesus Christ. For the sharing of this hope, the New Testament uniformly recognizes holiness as a necessity. According to Jesus, only the pure in heart will see God. According to John, the one who hopes to see the returning Christ and become fully like Him purifies himself as He is pure. And the writer of Hebrews insists that without sanctification no one shall see the Lord. Holiness is wedded to hope in the Word. This holiness is created and sustained by the Holy Spirit as He dwells in our hearts and works in our lives. His very inner presence should keep us reminded of the coming hour of judgment, "an hour when profession, with all its symbols and rituals, devoid of oil and light and power, will have no avail."[47]

If the parable of the 10 virgins warns us that we must be found ready at the coming of Jesus Christ, the passage from Zacharias' prophecy assures us that day-by-day holiness is a distinct possibility for the Christian.

---

45. Earle, op. cit., p. 225.
46. Cox, op. cit., pp. 149-50.
47. G. Campbell Morgan, *Parables and Metaphors*, p. 150.

2. Perseverance in holiness is a provision of divine grace in the new covenant

The father of John the Baptist blesses God for visiting His people in order to redeem them. This He does by raising up "a horn of salvation" for them "in the house of David," a reference to Jesus as the Messiah. "This image of a horn is frequent in the Old Testament, where it had been already applied to the Messiah: *I will raise up a horn to David* (Ps. cxxxii. 16)."[48] The horn was a figure for strength. "Just as the power of an animal is, as it were, concentrated in its horn, so all the redeeming power of God that was promised to the house of David will be concentrated in the Messiah-Redeemer."[49] Zacharias obviously refers to the imminent appearing of Christ, of whose nativity he had learned from Elisabeth (cf. vv. 39-56), and not to his son, for he was not of David's house.

The power of this Savior to deliver His people extends to their mightiest enemies. By "the hand of our enemies" the old priest may well have meant the Romans, who had subjugated the Jews. As Plummer says, "The tyranny of heathen conquerors was a hindrance to holiness."[50] Nonetheless, the greatest opposition to lives of holiness comes, not from external and physical factors, but from sin. Even if we grant that Zacharias probably envisioned "a liberation of Israel from political bonds," we are safe in affirming that "the principal meaning of these words, uttered under the inspiration of the Holy Ghost, is salvation from the guilt and power of sin."[51] It is the promise of a deliverance so radical

---

48. Godet, op. cit., p. 111.

49. Norval Geldenhuys, *Commentary on the Gospel of Luke,* New International Commentary on the New Testament (Grand Rapids: Wm. B. Eerdmans Publishing Co., 1956), p. 93.

50. Op. cit., p. 42.

51. Geldenhuys, op. cit., p. 93.

and enduring as to enable us to live holy and righteous lives "all our days."

The combination of "holiness and righteousness" occurs elsewhere in Scripture (cf. Eph. 4:24). Paul testifies to the quality of his own life in these terms (1 Thess. 2:10), and he urges it as a standard of character and behavior for elders in the Church (Titus 1:8). Godet distinguishes the first term as "a negative quality, the absence of stain," and the second as "a positive quality, the presence of all those religious and moral virtues which render worship acceptable to God."[52] A. B. Bruce gives both terms behavioral significance, describing "holiness" as "the Godward, religious aspect of conduct," and "righteousness" as "the manward, ethical aspect."[53] Charles Childers takes a similar position: "To serve God in holiness is to serve with an inward nature conformed to God's nature and will; to serve Him in righteousness is to serve in uprightness in all human and earthly relationships."[54]

Whatever nuances and shades of meaning we may posit for the two terms, they certainly point to an inward purity and outward integrity that keep one in favor with God, which only the redeeming grace and power of Jesus can establish. But His grace does establish it! Whatever the days of our lives, in their swift succession, may bring forth as testing and challenge, we can live and serve throughout them in holiness. The grace of God that makes us holy and keeps us holy does not "need to be spasmodic; it is intended to be an established mode of life."[55]

The hand of our enemies is strong and cruel. Sin, in its power, guilt, and stain, grips life at its very source to twist

---

52. Op. cit., p. 113.
53. *Expositor's Greek Testament*, p. 419.
54. Op. cit., p. 443.
55. Ibid.

it out of joint with the will of God. But if the hand of the enemy is strong, the "horn of salvation" is mightier yet! Jesus Christ, in fulfilling the covenant of God with Abraham and with David, has wrought a deliverance from sin that frees and purifies and strengthens us to serve God in holiness and righteousness. Such service is not a Sunday thing, not a revival meeting thing, but an everyday matter. Its character is not occasional but consistent.

Because this is true, the Christian can live in readiness for whatever the future brings, even if it brings the return of Jesus Christ.

* * *

Let us reflect now upon the preaching values of these scriptures in reference to our task of preaching holiness.

1. *The process of holiness must be emphasized as well as the crisis.* There is an inward cleansing from sin which is wrought in a moment of time as the divine response to a faith that embraces the promise of God to sanctify His people wholly. This we ought to continue to proclaim without stammering. But there have been people so fascinated with the gateway through which they entered that they have failed to give attention to the pilgrim pathway that leads on from it into a future of increasing likeness to Christ and usefulness in His service. The direction in which one is moving is of greater moment than any point at which he has arrived. If he keeps going on, he will pass through the crisis points of experience. But to loiter at the gate and fail to travel the road will lead to stagnation and failure. Continuing in the way of holiness needs to be pressed as duty and privilege upon our people. Not what we were 10 years ago, but what we are now is the vital issue!

2. *The necessity of constant readiness to meet Christ is an urgent note in biblical preaching.* While many moderns have repudiated this hope, denying it outright or explaining

it away, those who believe the Scriptures will expect Him to come again. This hope is designed to bless and comfort the people of God. When the preaching of Christ's second advent nearly scares the church out of its wits, something is terribly wrong about the way we preach it! And yet, the note of warning is valid, for this was Jesus' own accent in some of His teachings. If we are unprepared, as were the foolish virgins, we ought to fear, and fear enough to quickly remedy our lack. For when, like the prudent virgins, we have spiritual resources adequate for the event, we may anticipate His coming with joy. We may engage in the necessary and routine business of our daily lives, willing to have any and all of our plans interrupted by the midnight cry. Because the day and hour are still unmarked on our calendars, the only wisdom is consistent readiness through persevering holiness.

3. *The provision of God in Jesus Christ to make and keep us holy is a happy stress in our preaching.* We must lift up the drooping hands and strengthen the wobbly knees of tested and tried saints by pointing them away from their weakness and failure to His supply of the Spirit for "all our days." The days of unusually heavy work loads, the days of illness and grief and pain, the days of unexpected bad news, the days of swift bereavement and severe shock, the days of discouraging unemployment and mounting expenses, the days of unrelenting harassment by opposers of the faith, the days of fierce Satanic assault in lonely temptation, the days when His presence seems to elude us and we feel bereft in a meaningless universe—all such days through which we pass need not rob us of spiritual victory. In Jesus Christ, our God has visited and redeemed His people, to deliver from our enemies and to preserve us in holiness and righteousness!

Blue Mondays, bustling Saturdays, crowded Sundays, and all the days between are arenas of life in which we may

84

prove the power of His grace for every circumstance. He has promised to be with us all the days (Matt. 28:20, marg.). He is with us by the presence and power of His Spirit (John 14:16-18). And His Spirit, filling our hearts and cleansing our lives, is an inward power greater than all the outward pressure exerted against us by the world, the flesh, and the devil! The perseverance of the saints is the gracious provision of His covenant of redemption.

V

The Ethics of Holiness

A. The Life of Love

"You have heard that it was said, 'YOU SHALL LOVE YOUR NEIGHBOR, and hate your enemy.'

"But I say to you, love your enemies, and pray for those who persecute you

in order that you may be sons of your Father who is in heaven; for He causes His sun to rise on the evil and the good, and sends rain on the righteous and the unrighteous.

"For if you love those who love you, what reward have you? Do not even the tax-gatherers do the same?

"And if you greet your brothers only, what do you do more than others? Do not even the Gentiles do the same?

> *"Therefore you are to be perfect, as your heaven-*
> *ly Father is perfect"* (Matt. 5:43-48).

PARALLEL: Luke 6:35-36

> *But when the Pharisees heard that He had put the*
> *Sadducees to silence, they gathered themselves to-*
> *gether.*
> *And one of them, a lawyer, asked Him a question,*
> *testing Him,*
> *"Teacher, which is the great commandment in*
> *the Law?"*
> *And He said to him, "'YOU SHALL LOVE THE*
> LORD YOUR GOD WITH ALL YOUR HEART, AND WITH
> ALL YOUR SOUL, AND WITH ALL YOUR MIND.'
> *"This is the great and foremost commandment.*
> *"And a second is like it, 'YOU SHALL LOVE*
> YOUR NEIGHBOR AS YOURSELF.'
> *"On these two commandments depend the whole*
> *Law and the Prophets"* (Matt. 22:34-40).

PARALLEL: Mark 12:28-31

The life of holiness is a life of love—*agape* love. The love that Jesus commands from His followers is more than the love a man feels for his friend or bears toward his wife. It transcends every concept of sentiment or affection. Its pattern is the love which God has shown to men. Therefore, when the writers of the New Testament wanted to describe this love, they used a term unique in the literature of that era. Their word was *agape.* It is significant that heathen writers do not use this term at all. Heathen gods did not love their devotees as Yahweh loved Israel. Paganism's only experiences of love were on a human level. For its new discovery of love, Scripture had to employ a new vocabu-lary. *Agape* was adopted in the Septuagint and in the New Testament to indicate God's love for men and their respon-sive love for God.

The word *love* has become sadly profaned and coars-ened in our culture. Christian writers have found it increas-ingly necessary to employ the transliterated Greek word in their discussions in order to distinguish love of the highest kind from love in its basest perversions. Indeed, *agape* is now used so much that it is found in the English language dictionaries.

As we confront the Synoptic passages relevant to this study, we see at once the correlation of love and holiness. Jesus' words, "Therefore you are to be perfect, even as your heavenly Father is perfect," according to A. M. Hunter, recall "Lev. 19:2, 'Ye shall be holy: for I the Lord your God am holy,' with a clear echo of Deut. 18:13, 'Thou shalt be perfect with the Lord thy God.'"[1] We may express it thus: "Be holy" equals "be perfect" equals "love as God loves." This is traditional Wesleyan doctrine. Accused of teaching that "holiness consisted in a flow of joy," Wesley replied, "I constantly told you quite the contrary: I told you it was love; the love of God and our neighbor."[2] Accordingly, it will be our purpose in this chapter to look at the life of love by which the holiness of the Lord's people is expressed.

1. *Love means likeness to God*

As God is holy, and therefore we must be holy, so "God is love," and therefore we must love. What is involved in the holiness of love is our moral resemblance to the Father who made us and the Redeemer who saved us. As A. B. Bruce succinctly puts it, *"Noblesse oblige;* God's sons must be Godlike."[3]

This is the import of Jesus' words in the Sermon on the Mount: "I say to you, love your enemies, and pray for those who persecute you; *in order that you may be sons of your Father who is in heaven"* (emphasis mine). He is not saying

---

1. *A Pattern for Life* (Philadelphia: Westminster Press, 1965), p. 62.

2. *A Plain Account of Christian Perfection* (reprint ed., Kansas City: Beacon Hill Press of Kansas City, 1966), p. 13.

3. *The Expositor's Greek Testament,* 1:114.

that we are constituted the sons of God by our love, as though we earned God's favor by our deeds of kindness. The Synoptics, along with the entire New Testament, know that we enter God's family as He graciously adopts us when we repent of our sins and believe on Jesus Christ. Our relationship to God is established by faith. Our resemblance to God is exhibited by love. Loving does not make us sons of God; it only shows that we are His sons. By loving, our sonship is affirmed. By failing to love, it is denied. "In a human family if a son honours and obeys his father, he realizes his sonship. If he dishonours and disrespects him, he repudiates his sonship. So it is in the family of God."[4]

The word "perfect" has given much offense to many interpreters of the Scriptures. Certainly it cannot be pressed to mean that one is to be *as* perfect as God, any more than the command to be holy means that one is to be *as* holy as God. It means rather that we are to be perfect *as*, that is, perfect in the same manner, not in the same measure. Jesus is speaking "not of degrees of excellence but of the kind of excellence which was to distinguish His disciples and characterize His kingdom."[5] Bonnard is right in saying that the "perfection" of Matt. 5:48 "does not make men who love into demigods, nor even into exceptional personalities."[6] It simply marks them as like God in the way He acts toward men.

And yet, when we have insisted that "perfect" is to be understood of *kind* and not of *degree*, we must also admit that such love as Jesus commands does excel in degree the love shown by non-Christians. We are confronted here by "Christ's doctrine of the extra."[7] If your love extends only to "those who love you," you are no different from un-

---

4. Hunter, *A Pattern for Life*, p. 62.
5. Brown, op. cit., p. 36.
6. Op. cit., p. 246.
7. Hunter, *A Pattern for Life*, p. 62.

converted Gentiles and notorious tax collectors. It is one thing, and a heathen thing, to love those who like you and who are like you. It is quite another thing, and a Christian thing, to love those who are unlike you and who even dislike you! He is concerned that His disciples excel the unconverted in their love. "He does not wish them to be moral mediocrities."[8]

Even within the chosen nation, tradition had imposed an ungodlike limitation upon the commandment to love. "You have heard that it was said, 'YOU SHALL LOVE YOUR NEIGHBOR, and hate your enemy.'" The One who is incarnate Love knew that "hate your enemies" was no part of the original command of God, but the result of misinterpreting and thus perverting certain Old Testament passages. He therefore "repeated the Mosaic commandment of fraternal love, but annulled what tradition had taken to be its limits."[9]

The boundary of love cannot be drawn to exclude the enemy, not even the enemy actively persecuting a disciple of Christ. So far from hating, he is to show love by *praying* for the persecutor. "Prayer is the greatest and most far-reaching kindness, agape's most expressive and always possible proof."[10] You cannot do anyone a higher service than true prayer. Jesus is saying, therefore, Do your most and best for those who treat you the worst! Obviously, the injunction is impossible counsel if love means feeling a sentimental affection for someone! But "agape is not a sentimental feeling, but the intention of doing good."[11]

God, in His merciful love, sends sun and rain to bless both the evil and the good. By doing this He is neither senti-

---

8. A. B. Bruce, *Expositor's Greek Testament*, 1:115.
9. Ceslaus Spicq, *Agape in the New Testament* (St. Louis: B. Herder Book Co., 1963), 1:10.
10. Ibid.
11. Ibid.

mental toward sinners nor indifferent to their sins. But He displays *active goodwill* toward all men, whoever they are and whatever they do. He structures this goodwill into the very operation of nature as a witness to His catholic love. And we who are His sons are to exhibit the same active goodwill to everyone. "To return evil for good is the devil's way: to return good for good is man's: to return good for evil is God's."[12] We are, as disciples of Jesus, set upon the way of God, the way of perfect love. Love means likeness to God.

2. Love means obedience to law

At this point we are concerned especially with the second passage, Matt. 22:34-40. But before we turn our attention to it, take note that love as obedience to law is also taught in the former passage. There the Messiah-King is addressing His Messianic community, and He imposes His will upon their lives—"But *I say to you*, love your enemies." Those who heard the Sermon on the Mount "were amazed at His teaching; for He was teaching them as one having authority, and not as their scribes" (7:28-29). He was not a professor lecturing; He was a King commanding! His words are the law of His kingdom.

In the passage from Matthew 22, Jesus is accosted by "a lawyer," probably "a doctor especially competent in exegesis."[13] This lawyer addressed Jesus as "Teacher." But notice the section of Scripture following this passage (vv. 41-46). There Jesus is the Questioner, and His question concerns the *Lordship* of the Messiah, the Son of David. Jesus does not reply to this lawyer as one teacher to another. This is not an exchange of opinions, whatever the lawyer intended! Jesus speaks as the Messiah. He speaks as the Lord.

---

12. Hunter, *A Pattern for Life*, p. 62.
13. Spicq, op. cit., p. 27.

He is not simply repeating or quoting a commandment; He is issuing the command!

The lawyer's request is for "a summarizing concept of the law of God."[14] We can sympathize with the question when we recall that rabbis had divided the law into 613 precepts, 365 of which were negative prohibitions, 248 of which were positive injunctions. In addition to these "grand oracles . . . elaborate and manifold,"[15] there had developed such "a maze of interpretive opinion . . . the tradition of the elders . . . that even specialists in that field were at a loss to know which precepts were vitally important and which were only relatively so."[16] The scribes used the comparative terms "heavy" and "light," but which were which? "Which is the great commandment in the Law?" was indeed a reasonable question.

Jesus unhesitatingly replied: The commandment to love God with all one's heart, soul, and mind, quoted from Deut. 6:5, is "the great and foremost commandment." But it has a corollary in the command to love one's neighbor as oneself, cited from Lev. 19:18. These are two of a kind. On these two, "like a door on its hinges,"[17] "depend the whole Law and the Prophets."

Thus, with Messianic authority, Jesus supplied the summarizing concept requested. In the "first" and "second" commandments we have "all Scripture in a nutshell."[18] "Law and . . . Prophets" was itself a summary phrase. Jesus said, in effect, "The moral drift of the whole O. T. is love."[19] Paul, taught by his Lord, echoes this in Romans:

---

14. J. Glenn Gould, *The Whole Counsel of God* (Kansas City: Beacon Hill Press, 1945), p. 15.

15. Ibid.

16. Ibid.

17. Stagg, op. cit., p. 209.

18. Brown, op. cit., p. 188.

19. A. B. Bruce, *The Expositor's Greek Testament*, 1:277.

"Love . . . is the fulfillment of the law" (13:10).

Spicq observes that the answer of Jesus "unified all morality, first by basing it entirely on exclusive adoration and worship of God (religious morality), then by consecrating Christians to the service of their brothers in the name of the love they bear God (social morality), and finally by requiring of each soul a single attitude, a single interior disposition—charity (individual morality)."[20] The tendency of men is to define, and seek to preserve, holiness by the multiplication of rules. Jesus does it by the reduction of multiple laws to a single category of human response—love God supremely and man unselfishly.

The command to love God is quoted from the *Shema*, the daily confession of faith made by devout Jews as the expression of "their central article of faith, the unity and holiness of God."[21] Holiness in God means that He is one. Holiness in Israel meant undivided love for Him.

This love was to be given with all the heart, soul, and might. Matthew has heart, soul, and mind. Mark adds "strength." One can easily read too much into the separate terms, since they are used in the Old Testament in virtually synonymous ways. They stand for the full inner life, all that a man is. "What is intended in each passage is the whole self given to God and others."[22]

Such love is "more a service than a sentiment."[23] The Bible knows nothing of love as an emotional activity divorced from volitional activity. Love can almost be equated with obedience. "To love God is to serve Him," and the *Shema*, from which Jesus quotes, is bracketed with injunctions to keep the commandments of the Lord (Deut. 5:28—6:3, 10-24). "You shall walk in all the way which the

---

20. Op. cit., pp. 31-32.
21. Cox, op. cit., p. 137.
22. Stagg, op. cit., p. 209.
23. Bonnard, op. cit., p. 245.

93

Lord your God has commanded you" is precisely equivalent to "You shall love the Lord your God with all your heart" (cf. Exod. 20:6; Deut. 5:10; 7:9; 11:1; 1 Kings 3:3; Neh. 1:5; Dan. 9:4). Jesus, foremost Interpreter of Holy Writ, makes the same identification of love with obedience: "If you love Me, you will keep My commandments" (John 14: 15; cf. 15:10; 1 John 5:2-3).

The love one has for the neighbor is not another kind of love than the love he has for God. "It is one love with two distinct objects,"[24] and with two distinct expressions. Towards God this love is expressed in *obedience*. Towards one's neighbor it is expressed in *service*. But in both cases it is one love. "Love cannot be divided, and the true self cannot be isolated from God or neighbor. Either one loves God, neighbor, and himself or he loves neither."[25] John, taught by Jesus what it means to love God and men, flatly brands as liar the one who claims to love God while he hates his brother (1 John 4:20-21). Since both are commanded, any failure to love man, whether one's "neighbor," "brother," or "enemy," is disobedience to God.

Furthermore, love cannot be a matter of words, but is always a matter of deeds. This is the plain teaching of Jesus, who said, "Love your enemies, *do good* to those who hate you, *bless* those who curse you, *pray* for those who mistreat you" (Luke 6:27-28). The "be . . . perfect" in love of Matt. 5:48 becomes "be . . . merciful" in Luke 6:36. With his penchant for terse definition, Stagg says, "Love is the basic disposition of one's whole being to relate to God for his glory and to man for his good."[26]

Sentimental affection cannot be commanded by law, but active goodwill can! And love, as the expression of holi-

24. Spicq, op. cit., p. 29.
25. Stagg, op. cit., p. 210.
26. Ibid., p. 209.

ness, is obedience to God's law. But love is not a matter of keeping the law in order to be saved. It means observing the law as the response of a heart grateful for salvation.

3. Love means dependence upon grace

Ralph Earle trenchantly says, "It is natural to love one's friends; it is supernatural to love one's enemies."[27] Before man can keep the commandments of love for God and others his heart must be transformed. The Old Testament teaches this in the promise, "And the Lord your God will circumcise your heart . . . so that you will love the Lord your God with all your heart and with all your soul, that you may live" (Deut. 30:6). This promise looks to the eschatological Kingdom for its fulfillment. It has long been regarded as Messianic. It is often linked, therefore, to Jer. 31:31-34, where a new covenant is promised to Israel, incorporating the forgiveness of sins and the inscribing of the law "upon their hearts."

In a related passage, Ezek. 36:22-27, this new covenant and new heart are seen as a vindication of God's holiness, and as a result of an infilling with the Spirit who causes the law to be obeyed. These passages have their fulfillment in Jesus Christ, the Messiah, in whose life and work the new age has begun, and who baptizes His people with the Holy Spirit, resulting in a cleansing of the heart from sin and an energizing of the life for obedience (cf. Matt. 3:11; Acts 2:4; 15:8-9; 1 Pet. 1:22; etc.).

As long as the heart is sinful and self-centered, the love for God and men commanded by Jesus remains impossible. But He can purify the heart, filling it with the Spirit, and thus enable His disciples to bear an honest resemblance to

---

27. Op. cit., p. 79.

the Father in the catholicity and compassion of their love for others.

* * *

And now, some attention to the preaching values of these passages is in order.

1. *Love as the unifying summary of law is important for us today.* Like Israel of old, we are prone to fix attention upon numerous moral laws, and multiply rules in the effort to interpret and apply the laws. Our moral earnestness, our very desire to be holy people, can betray us into casuistry and turn us into present-day Pharisees. Having multiplied the rules and elaborated the laws, we are tempted to think we can achieve holiness by scrupulously observing the moral system created. The effort to enforce holiness from the outside in must always terminate in despair or pride, alike destructive of genuine spirituality.

Holiness is love for God and others. If we truly love, we will not flout the law, for the essence of love towards God is obedience. And neither will we wrong our fellows, for the essence of love towards men is active goodwill. The law will take care of itself if the heart is cleansed and filled with overflowing love. Not a long list of rules, subject to endless debate that often sinks to petty quibbling, but a burning love that intends God's glory and man's good, this is our crying need. Then, and only then, can laws and rules become the structured life of holiness, the channels through which love flows, and not a substitute for holy love.

2. *Love as obedience to God and service to men is a needed emphasis, also.* Love has its vertical dimension, a truth in danger of neglect in our current emphasis on social activism. But it has also its horizontal dimensions, a truth that ' as been overlooked by those who sought to achieve holiness by avoiding social contact. The holy man is not a hermit, fixing attention upon God to the exclusion of men.

Nor is he a mere humanist, addressing himself to social needs without devotion to God. He is a Christian loving as Jesus loved, giving obedience to God wholeheartedly, and lending assistance to men unselfishly.

Love combines worship and work. In both cases, love is something we do, not just something we feel. Love is active, positive, moving towards its object. When God loves He sends sun and rain—and Jesus! When we love as He loves, we actively promote the welfare of others. This means that love will keep us in the fellowship of the saints when they gather for worship. And it will make us part of the Church as well when it is scattered to witness, by words and deeds, out in the world where men sin and toil and bleed and die. Love is neither private morality nor public charity to the exclusion of one another; it is both of them at once.

3. *Love as a possibility of grace needs proclamation.* The love commandment of Jesus is too often shrugged off as impractical idealism. And man, in his own resources, cannot measure up to the demand. But the people of the Lord can be filled with the Spirit! The indwelling Spirit cleanses from sin, which is basically self-centeredness, the very antithesis of agape. Thus the Spirit of Christ, ruling in our hearts, produces the fruit of love and enables us to relate to God for His glory and to men for their good.

There is an ethical pessimism in much modern theology that is unwarranted by Scripture. The Lord intends that we shall live lives of perfect (that is, catholic) love. He provides the dynamic for conducting our lives in love. The Master said, "If you then, being evil, know how to give good gifts to your children, how much more shall your Heavenly Father give the Holy Spirit to those who ask Him?" (Luke 11:13). Why do we human fathers give good things to our children? To enable them, in a material sense, to live both happily and adequately. And God gives the Holy Spirit to make possible, in spiritual dimensions, a life of adequacy and victory—

97

which is another way of saying, a life of love. R. N. Flew is correct in his insistence that "Jesus spoke to men as though in their doing of the will of God they had all the powers and gifts of the Kingdom of God on their side. Chief among these was the gift of the Spirit of God."[28] His words can be translated into our deeds by the power of His sanctifying Spirit!

The heart can be circumcised to make love for God a wholehearted possibility (cf. Rom. 2:29; Col. 2:11-13). In the "freely justified, wholly sanctified, increasingly transformed" complex of Christian experience we are enabled to love God, our neighbor, and ourselves, and even our enemies. Stephen, an ordinary flesh-and-blood Christian like ourselves, was able to die at the hands of merciless tormentors, praying in reminiscence of Calvary love, "Lord, do not hold this sin against them!" How could he love like that? He was "full of the Holy Spirit" (Acts 7:55-60). If the Spirit can enable a Christian to die loving, He can also enable a Christian to live loving!

B. The Life of Purity

> "Blessed are the pure in heart, for they shall see God" (Matt. 5:8).
>
> "The lamp of the body is the eye; if therefore your eye is clear, your whole body will be full of light.
>
> "But if your eye is bad, your whole body will be full of darkness. If therefore the light that is in you is darkness, how great is the darkness!
>
> "No one can serve two masters; for either he will hate the one and love the other, or he will hold to one and despise the other. You cannot serve God and mammon" (Matt. 6:22-24).

PARALLEL: Luke 11:34-36

---

28. *Jesus and His Way* (London: Epworth Press, 1963), p. 57.

> *And a leper came to Him, beseeching Him and falling on his knees before Him, and saying to Him, "If You are willing, You can make me clean."*
>
> *And moved with compassion, He stretched out His hand and touched him, and said to him, "I am willing; be cleansed."*
>
> *And immediately the leprosy left him and he was cleansed* (Mark 1:40-42).
>
> PARALLELS: Matt. 8:2-4; Luke 5:12-14

Holiness, in God, is more than moral purity, but it is not less. Even so, holiness in God's people is broader than moral purity but includes it. The life of holiness is a life of purity.

To speak of life in biblical terms is to speak of the heart, not merely of the behavior. "Keep your heart with all vigilance;" said the writer of Proverbs, "for from it flow the springs of life" (Prov. 4:23). Jesus located moral defilement, not in external factors, but in the heart. "Out of the heart come evil thoughts, murders, adulteries, fornications, thefts, false witness, slanders. These are the things which defile the man" (Matt. 15:19-20). Purity cannot be merely a matter of outward conformity to moral laws or religious customs. It must first of all be a condition of the inner life. The ethics of the kingdom of God is "a morality of the heart."[29]

To discuss the pure life, then, we go to the very heart of all passages about the heart, the sixth beatitude: "Blessed are the pure in heart, for they shall see God."

To enter into the meaning of this verse of Scripture, we need to recognize its Jewishness. Jesus is the Messiah who brings in the kingdom of God. Here He was addressing the disciples who were the nucleus of His Messianic community. The Sermon on the Mount has been aptly called "a design for life in the Kingdom of God."[30] In these Beatitudes

---

29. A. B. Bruce, *The Training of the Twelve* (New York: A. C. Armstrong and Son, 1908), p. 43.

30. Hunter, *A Pattern for Life*, p. 114.

with which the great sermon begins, Jesus is using words, and using them in ways with which He and His disciples were familiar from reading their Bible, the Old Testament. The language of the Beatitudes was "purposely fetched from the Old Testament,"[31] and describes character that was the real essence of genuine spirituality throughout the ages.

We need to pose these questions, therefore: What does "heart" mean in Hebrew psychology? What does "purity" signify to those who are schooled on the Old Testament? And how would Jesus and His disciples understand the notion of "seeing" God?

1. The meaning of heart

Anyone who studies the Old Testament usage of "heart" (the Hebrew is *leb*) will be amazed at the number of times it occurs and the variety of meanings it has. Of course the ancient writers knew the heart as a physical organ. And because emotional reactions were accompanied by felt changes in the rate and rhythm of pulsation, "heart" was used to describe the emotional activities. But it was employed far more frequently with the activities of the intellect and the will. Its connection with the intellectual and volitional processes is what gives "heart" its "distinctive stamp in Hebrew thought. . . . It is the conscious and deliberate spiritual activity of the self-contained human ego which is meant."[32] In short, the heart stood for the entire inner life, the capacity and energy of a person to feel, think, and resolve, with emphasis on the thinking and willing.

Transplanted to the soil of the New Testament, the word retained the same comprehensiveness and the same emphasis. In the heart, sin is committed (Matt. 5:22, 28). In the heart forgiveness is granted (Matt. 18:35). In the heart con-

---

31. Brown, op. cit., p. 25.
32. Eichrodt, op. cit., 2:143.

demnation is felt (1 John 3:20). In the heart thought is formed (Mark 7:21; Luke 2:19). In the heart speech is born (Matt. 12:34-37). In the heart obedience is given (Rom. 6: 17). Doubt (Mark 11:23), decision (2 Cor. 9:7), deception (Jas. 1:26), belief (Rom. 10:9), sorrow (John 16:6), illumination (2 Cor. 4:6), and assurance (1 John 3:19) are all affairs of the heart. After studying the usage of "heart" in both Testaments, Owen Brandon says, "The NT word *kardia* reproduces and expands the ideas included in the OT words *leb* and *lebab*."[33] And the great lexicographer F. Wilbur Gingrich defines the Greek word for heart "mainly as the center and source of the whole inner life."[34]

2. *The meaning of purity*

The breadth of meaning that attaches to "heart" at once cautions us not to unduly restrict the meaning of purity. A British scholar complains against the limitation put on the words "pure in heart" in much modern usage. "We tend to think only of freedom from lustful thoughts, the absence of sensual defilement."[35] No one can deny that this aspect of purity is important, especially in a culture that has idolized sex! But in the thought of Jesus, "pure" certainly has a more positive and expansive meaning.

The Greek word for "pure," transliterated, is *katharos.* In the Septuagint it has more than 150 occurrences, and the majority of these have to do with ceremonial purity—describing people, places, and things which are clean in the sense of meeting the ritual requirements of the law. Less frequently, but more importantly, the term *katharos* is

---

33. *Baker's Dictionary of Theology,* "Heart" (Grand Rapids: Baker Book House, 1960), p. 262.

34. *Shorter Lexicon of the Greek New Testament* (Chicago: University of Chicago Press, 1965), p. 107.

35. Flew, op. cit., p. 50.

employed to designate moral and spiritual cleanness (e.g., Gen. 20:5-6; Job 4:7; Ps. 24:4; 51:10; Isa. 1:16; Hab. 1:13). In such cases it refers to the integrity, uprightness, blamelessness, and uncompromised truth of one's thought and behavior.

The external, ceremonial purity was "the official and orthodox conception of purity in the time of Jesus."[36] We meet it constantly in the Pharisees. But in making purity a matter of the heart, of the inner life, Jesus decisively contradicted and repudiated the Pharisaic viewpoint as an impoverished conception. He insisted upon internal, moral purity by which the whole inner life is to be governed.

When the moral-usage instances of the word are explored, they have a common denominator. They carry the idea of that which is pure because it contains no foreign admixture. Pure food contains no filth or poison. Pure metal contains no dross or alloys. Pure wool contains no cotton fibers. Pure air contains no smog. Pure nonsense contains no logic. We conclude that in the sixth beatitude our Lord "describes the bliss of the heart whose thoughts, motives, desires are completely unmixed, genuine, sincere."[37]

We have said that the distinctive stamp of the Hebrew usage of "heart" is its intellectual and volitional emphasis. This being so, most scholars think of heart purity as "singlemindedness," in contrast to "a double-minded man, unstable in all his ways" (Jas. 1:8).[38] Thus, for example, in his exegetical study of *katharos*, Friedrich Hauck says, "The purity of the NT community is personal and moral by nature. It consists in full and unreserved self-offering to

---

36. Wm. Barclay, *The Beatitudes and the Lord's Prayer for Everyman* (New York: Harper & Row, 1964), p. 80.

37. Ibid.

38. See Filson, op. cit., p. 78.

God which renews the heart and rules out any acceptance of what is against God."[39]

Understood in this way, the pure heart is almost synonymous with the "single eye" that Jesus speaks about elsewhere in the Sermon on the Mount (6:22-24). The single eye, by which the whole body is lighted, means that "singleness of purpose, or purity of intention"[40] which keeps a person from dividing his loyalty between God and mammon. We have seen earlier that exclusive devotion to God was the essence of Israel's holiness as a nation. It is this same kind of undivided allegiance that Jesus commends in the sixth beatitude. "The pure in heart are the singleminded who are free from the tyranny of a divided self, and who do not try to serve God and the world at the same time."[41] Insofar as the words of Jesus can be construed as a promise, they are the answer to two prayers heard in the Psalms. The first is, "Create in me a clean heart, O God" (Ps. 51:10). The second is, "Unite my heart to fear thy name" (Ps. 86:11).

To summarize our thinking thus far, the heart is the entire inner life, and purity is wholeness, undividedness, unmixedness. Frank Stagg puts it all together in a choice definition: "Purity of heart is simplicity or integrity as against duplicity. It is the concentration of the whole self upon God."[42]

3. The meaning of seeing God

When Moses cried, "Show me thy glory," God answered, "You cannot see my face; for man shall not see me and live" (Exod. 33:18-23). The holiness of God stands in

---

39. *Theological Dictionary of the New Testament,* 3:425.
40. Earle, op. cit., p. 85.
41. Tasker, op. cit., p. 62.
42. Op. cit., p. 105.

awful contrast to the fallenness of man, and seeing the unveiled splendor of God would blind and destroy frail flesh! For that reason the vision of God is represented in the Old Testament as a reward that awaits the removal of every human deficiency, especially sin, but also its vitiating effects upon the body and mind. The vision lies beyond death and resurrection. Thus the Psalmist says, "As for me, I shall behold thy face in righteousness; when I awake, I shall be satisfied with beholding thy form" (Ps. 17:15).

Yet Moses was permitted to see a partial disclosure of God's glory, and the Old Testament knows a sense in which men see God in this life. The Psalmist exclaims, "I have looked upon thee in the sanctuary, beholding thy power and glory" (Ps. 63:2; cf. 27:4). From such references we conclude that to see God "meant to a Jew 'to appear before God,' especially in worship. The qualification for this is no mere freedom from ceremonial defilement, but singleminded service."[43] "Who shall stand in his holy place?" the Psalmist asks, and then replies, "He who has clean hands and a pure heart" (24:3-4; thought by most to have influenced Matt. 5:8).

The New Testament preserves this concept of seeing God as future and yet somehow present. The final reward of the pure in heart is described in Revelation: "They shall see His face" (22:4). This will take place in heaven, "all veils of sin and sense removed"[44] by the resurrection. For that beatific vision holiness is mandatory (Heb. 12:14; 1 John 3:2).

But in the New Testament there is also presented the possibility of a partial fulfillment of that promise of seeing God (2 Cor. 3:18). Because the eschatological kingdom of God has already come in Jesus Christ, and because the life

---

43. Cox, op. cit., p. 47.
44. Hunter, *A Pattern for Life*, p. 40.

104

of that Kingdom has already begun for those in Christ (5: 17), there can be a present anticipation and partial realization of the final reward of seeing God (4:6; 1 John 3:6; 3 John 11). As R. Newton Flew has said, "Jesus Christ captured the present tense for religion, while keeping the full force of the future tense unimpaired."[45]

As in the Old Testament, so in the New, the present vision of God is related to worship, communion, and fellowship. "It is not a matter of optics," as Hunter puts it, "but of spiritual fellowship."[46] The fellowship which man has with Christ is morally conditioned. It requires purity of heart. "Sin is like dust in the eyes. It beclouds the vision and distorts the view. We can enter into full communion with the Lord only when our hearts are cleansed from all sin (cf. 1 John 1:7)."[47]

Purity of heart is a present possibility. This is the unmistakable implication of Jesus' words. But in the case of men, *katharos* must mean that which is pure because it has been purified. We are not pure in heart by nature. Rather, we are corrupt and defiled. We must be cleansed, and we cannot effect this cleansing ourselves (Job 14:4; Ps. 51:5, 10; Jer. 17:9). As the Psalmist became aware of his deep inward pollution, he despaired of any cleansing except by the creative power of God himself. The apostles knew that the Lord alone who spoke this beatitude could bring about within men the purity it describes.

This cleansing power of Jesus is happily illustrated in the healing of the leper, told about in Mark 1:40-42.

Older exegetes often spoke of leprosy as a type of sin, and of the leper as the type of one dead in sin. The leper in his misery and the bereaved in his mourning employed the

---

45. Op. cit., p. 23.
46. *A Pattern for Life*, p. 39.
47. Earle, op. cit., p. 70.

105

same symbols for the expression of grief and the ceremonies of cleansing. In the moral education of Israel, according to Brown, leprosy was "a familiar and effective symbol of sin, considered as (1) loathsome, (2) spreading, (3) incurable." [48]

In more recent times this position has been virtually abandoned. A famous volume of biblical studies flatly declared, "The homiletic use of leprosy as a type of sin is not Biblical." [49]

Be that as it may, the physical blight and the social plight of the leper in Bible times may fittingly serve us as an illustration of the defiling and deteriorating effects of sin. And the healing of this leper may surely illustrate the willingness and power of Jesus Christ to save men from the sin which corrupts and alienates.

I am particularly interested in the fact that Jesus touched the leper. For it is by the Holy Spirit that our hearts are purified (Acts 15:8-9); and the Spirit, as we considered earlier, is the Power by which God acts upon man at the point of his need. Jesus taught that His healing and saving miracles, wrought by the Holy Spirit, were the result of "the finger of God" touching human life (Luke 11:20; Matt. 12:28). God sent His Son, who sends His Spirit into our hearts as a flaming and welding Presence to cleanse and to unite them, so that we may have undivided love and loyalty for God.

* * *

What are the specific lessons for us here as we face the task of preaching holiness?

1. *The priority given to the heart is instructive.* It is, after all, just as easy for men to become externalists and

---

48. Op. cit., p. 51.
49. Alex Macalister, *The International Standard Bible Encyclopaedia*, 3:1867.

formalists today as it was in Jesus' day. The temptation to substitute symbols and rituals for the reality of spiritual life is always present. To feel that because one goes to church, says his prayers, takes the sacraments, pays his tithes, and refrains from dynamiting the parsonage when he disagrees with the preaching, he is therefore holy, is not a capital mistake made only by ancient Pharisees. We need to confront those under our care with the all-importance of a clean and steadfast heart, fixed on God and yielded to His will. Nothing, but nothing, is of greater urgency than the healing and health of the very springs of life.

2. *The possibility of purity, here and now, as a foretaste of the life of eternity is a needed emphasis.* Theology in this century has swung from the extreme naivete of those who denied the heart's innate depravity and need for redemptive cleansing to the extreme pessimism of those who so concentrated upon the rootedness of sin that they despaired of any actual cleansing in this life. The New Testament does not have a sin-fixation but a grace-fixation! This beatitude is a choice place to stand and, without blinking the horror and depth of sin, proclaim the sanctifying might of the Redeemer!

3. *Men need to see God, not only in the future of eternity, but in whatever sense and degree that vision is possible now.* It is the only vision that gives hope to our plundered planet and weary race. Men see themselves, and the sight is one of sin, failure, heartache, and emptiness that leaves them frustrated, cheerless, lonely, and afraid. Men see the times, and the sight of war, crime, violence, revolution, and bloodletting leaves them shattered and hopeless. Men see the world, and the sight of air pollution, soil pollution, and water pollution fills them with despair for the sheer survival of humankind. As long as the horizon lacks a God-dimension, as long as our knowledge is limited to dwindling material and human resources, our misery must go un-

relieved. When men are fixed up to see God, they discover who they really are, what their earth really means, and what their society really ought to become. Value, beauty, and purpose are born of hope. We are to summon men to a redeeming encounter with God that will prepare their hearts to see Him who is the only true Life and Future for us all.

4. *The ultimate future of the saints*, the face-to-face communion with God that awaits us, *is a needed message to comfort God's people as they pass through tribulation.* To know that we shall see Him, beyond all the veils, trammels, and interruptions we now experience, and that we shall never again be hidden from His face, makes all the sufferings of discipleship but light afflictions. People are serving God under intense pressure and heavy burdens. They need constant reminders that the joy and peace and glory of His presence now are just a fragment of that bliss we shall know after a while. Thinking upon that final reward will brace and nerve the servants of God for every task assigned them and every trial experienced by them. Give your people courage and heart by proclaiming the biblical future as their hope!

C. The Life of Service

> *And behold, a certain lawyer stood up and put Him to the test, saying, "Teacher, what shall I do to inherit eternal life?"*
>
> *And He said to him, "What is written in the Law? How does it read to you?"*
>
> *And he answered and said,* "YOU SHALL LOVE THE LORD YOUR GOD WITH ALL YOUR HEART, AND WITH ALL YOUR SOUL, AND WITH ALL YOUR STRENGTH, AND WITH ALL YOUR MIND; AND YOUR NEIGHBOR AS YOURSELF."
>
> *And He said to him, "You have answered correctly;* DO THIS, AND YOU WILL LIVE."
>
> *But wishing to justify himself, he said to Jesus, "And who is my neighbor?"*

Jesus replied and said, "A certain man was going down from Jerusalem to Jericho; and he fell among robbers, and they stripped him and beat him, and went off leaving him half dead.

"And by chance a certain priest was going down on that road, and when he saw him, he passed by on the other side.

"And likewise a Levite also, when he came to the place and saw him, passed by on the other side.

"But a certain Samaritan, who was on a journey, came upon him; and when he saw him, he felt compassion,

and came to him, and bandaged up his wounds, pouring oil and wine on them; and he put him on his own beast, and brought him to an inn, and took care of him.

"And on the next day he took out two denarii and gave them to the innkeeper and said, 'Take care of him; and whatever more you spend, when I return, I will repay you.'

"Which of these three do you think proved to be a neighbor to the man who fell into the robbers' hands?"

And he said, "The one who showed mercy toward him." And Jesus said to him, "Go and do the same" (Luke 10:25-37).

Writing to Timothy, the apostle Paul said, "The goal of our instruction is love from a pure heart" (1 Tim. 1:5). When men turn aside from this, the result is "fruitless discussion" (v. 6). Jesus insisted, as we have already seen, upon the priorities of love and purity in His teaching. That He would not make these simply the subject of fruitless discussion is vividly borne out in the story of the good Samaritan. His closing charge is, "Go and do." The lawyer with whom He dialogued was quite willing to keep the whole matter in the area of academic discussion, but Jesus is concerned about decisive and responsible living—doing the truth.

This means that holiness is not simply love and purity in abstraction from life, a static condition maintained in isolation from human needs. True Christian love and purity issue in deeds, in service, in positive response to the hurt life all around us. The life of holiness is a life of service! Nowhere is this fact better expressed than in the story of the good Samaritan.

A lawyer approached Jesus and "put Him to the test." The Greek text contains "a technical term for asking a difficult scholarly question, to establish by it whether the man questioned is a real scholar."[50] Jesus had gained considerable notoriety as an itinerant rabbi. Now the "novice" is being challenged by the "pro" who seeks to test His ability as a teacher. The test question was a standard one, and we cannot really know the extent to which the lawyer was actually involved in the issue raised. "Teacher, what shall I do to inherit eternal life?"

Jesus had a disturbing way of answering questions with questions (cf. Matt. 22:15-46). "What is written in the Law? How does it read to you?" In other words, "You are the expert. What is your answer?" And the lawyer's answer was right, as he brought together the two greatest commandments: "You shall love the Lord your God with all your heart . . . and your neighbor as yourself." Elsewhere in the Gospels these two commandments, cited from separate sources in the Pentateuch, are synthesized by Jesus himself. One suspects that the lawyer had heard this and approved, as did another lawyer on another occasion (Mark 12:28-34). Jesus, having neatly reversed the situation, gives the veteran teacher a passing grade! "You have answered correctly." But He continues with another citation from the law that takes the discussion out of a merely intellectual atmosphere into

---

50. K. Bornhauser, quoted by Eta Linnemann, *Parables of Jesus* (London: SPCK, 1966), p. 50.

an existential one: "Do this, and you will live" (cf. Lev. 18: 5).

"Wishing to justify himself," the lawyer posed another question. "And who is my neighbor?" How far do the boundaries of love extend? Jesus replied with a story, one of the best-known and hardest-hitting stories He ever told.

We are not told with whom the lawyer wished to justify himself. Some think, in the eyes of the encircling crowd. Others think, in the eyes of his peer group, his fellow instructors in the law. G. Campbell Morgan says, "With his own conscience. He was dodging an issue."[51] If this was so, Jesus left him very little room to dodge!

Jesus knew, and the lawyer knew, what the "orthodox" answer to his question was. "It was generally agreed," wrote Jeremias, "that the term connoted fellow-countrymen, including full proselytes."[52] But various groups of Jewish teachers wanted to draw the circle of responsibility even closer than this! Thus, "the Pharisees were inclined to exclude non-Pharisees; the Essenes required that a man 'should hate all the sons of darkness'; a rabbinical saying rules that heretics, informers, and renegades 'should be pushed [into the ditch] and not pulled out,' and a widespread popular saying excepted personal enemies."[53]

Up to a point, the story permitted the apprehensive lawyer some degree of relaxation. A man, presumably a Jew, is robbed, beaten, and left dying on the notorious bandit-infested road that leads down from Jerusalem to Jericho. Passing by, first a priest and then a Levite see the wretched victim but refuse to do anything to help. They callously go on their way. Other matters are more important. But as long as some Jew comes by and assists the wretch, the story will

---

51. *Parables and Metaphors*, p. 178.
52. Jeremias, op. cit., pp. 202-3.
53. Ibid.

end on a satisfactory note. But Jesus introduces "a certain Samaritan," and one can easily imagine the gasps and murmurs that caused! If anyone was not a neighbor in Jewish eyes, it was a Samaritan. Bitter hostility existed between them, and it was mutual. Oesterley notes that "a petition was daily offered up" by the Jews "praying God that the Samaritans might not be partakers of eternal life."[54] You cannot hate more deeply than this, that you desire the damnation of another!

But love reached farther than hate. The Samaritan dressed the man's wounds, placed him on his own "beast," took him to an inn, and left him in the care of the innkeeper, footing the expenses himself. He did all that he could do for the sufferer.

Then Jesus smites the conscience of the lawyer, converting the question to: "Which of these three do you think proved to be a neighbor to the man who fell into the robbers' hands?" There can be just one answer, and the lawyer gives it. But how far short his neighbor love falls is betrayed by the very phrasing of his reply. Had the priest or Levite been the hero of the story he would gladly have said, "The priest," or, "The Levite." But he cannot bring himself to say, "The Samaritan." "As his heart refuses to pronounce the word Samaritan with praise, he paraphrases the odious name,"[55] and lamely responds, "The one who showed mercy toward him." Then Jesus spoke with all the authority of His Lordship, and not as one teacher to another, "Go and do the same." We can only hope that the lawyer obeyed!

Out of this story arises the emphatic truth that the life of holiness is a life of service—love-inspired service.

---

54. W. O. E. Oesterley, *The Gospel Parables in the Light of Their Jewish Backgrounds* (London: SPCK, 1936), p. 162.

55. Godet, op. cit., p. 41.

1. *Official holiness is no substitute for personal holiness*

A. B. Bruce describes the moral of Jesus' story in the terse phrase, "Charity the true sanctity." And he says of the priest and Levite that they were "persons holy by profession and occupation."[56] It is true that in Jesus' day, the priests were not popularly regarded as the examples of holiness in Israel; rather the Pharisees and scribes were the "holy men." Nevertheless, by virtue of their office they were holy, and they were supposed to be in fact what they were in word.

The priest in Israel was not elected by the people nor was he self-appointed to the office. "Divine selection severed him from those for whom he was to act."[57] This very divine severance involves the idea of apartness which was an element in holiness. The priest was a separated person. Furthermore, "the ordination of priests was the occasion of a solemn ceremony, the object of which was to confirm that they belonged to a special domain, that of the holy"[58] (cf. Exod. 28:41; 30:30; Lev. 8:12-13). The whole content of the Old Testament record of the choosing, investiture, and performances of the priest emphasizes that he is "a sacred person . . . specially connected with the supremely holy God."[59] The Levites were subordinate priests, and also holy by office.

That any priest should regard holiness as primarily a matter of ritual and profession only shows how little he truly knew the God to whom he stood in special connection. The God of Israel was a God who loved, and whose love was expressed in deeds, namely, the divine acts of election, re-

---

56. *The Parabolic Teaching of Christ*, p. 345.
57. Wm. G. Moorehead, "Priest," *The International Standard Bible Encyclopaedia*, 4:2439.
58. G. Pidoux, "Priesthood," *A Companion to the Bible*, p. 340.
59. Ibid.

demption, and preservation by which the nation had its existence. The holiness of that God could not be truly mirrored in any loveless life, or in any life that reduced love to mere sentiment or that restricted love to one's fellows. "God has no higher life than that of love."[60] Therefore the commandments to love God and one's neighbor, in the teaching of Jesus, "are the result neither of logical analysis of the *Torah* nor of a process of selection by personal preference. They are commandments which actually take precedence of every other. For Jesus these two are in a class by themselves. . . . They enjoy priority, not logical or relative, but absolute."[61] In short, to apply any commandment in a way that circumvents the full meaning of these two is a perversion and violation of the law, for it obscures the real meaning of God's holy love.

Special pleading has been done for the priest on the grounds of his devotion to duty at the Temple. To have come into contact with what he thought was a dead body would have rendered him ceremonially unclean, preventing him from serving his turn in the house of worship. Or he may have been hurrying to that task and felt it of such importance that it took priority over the needs of the badly wounded victim of crime. But there is no possible ground for justifying the action of the priest and Levite. God loves, loves all men, loves them with a serving love. To pass by and do nothing for someone who requires assistance is a denial of God. No measure of scrupulosity with regard to ceremonies of worship can have precedence over human need. No expression of official holiness can have the value of personal holiness which shows itself in love-doing for others. "The Scriptures teach that without holiness no man

60. Godet, op. cit., p. 39.
61. T. W. Manson, *The Teaching of Jesus* (Cambridge: The University Press, 1948), p. 301.

shall see the Lord, that is, have eternal life; and in this parable two kinds of holiness are set before us, the one spurious, the other genuine. The spurious . . . sanctity divorced from charity . . . genuine holiness . . . the practice of charity."[62]

2. The service of holy love ignores the boundaries imposed by the prejudices, bigotries, and hates of men

The lawyer who questioned Jesus and the Samaritan in the story had one thing in common—the Scriptures from which the law of love was quoted. In postexilic times the Samaritans were not permitted to share the rebuilding or the worship services of the Temple, being despised as half-breeds. They reacted in anger, seeking to frustrate the construction project and setting up a rival place of worship on Mount Gerizim. Through the intervening centuries, the hostilities deepened to the point that calling a Jew "a Samaritan" was a gross insult (cf. John 8:48). But the Samaritans had their copies of the Pentateuch, which they regarded as the Word of God, although they did not accept the other books of the Old Testament. From his incomplete Bible this Samaritan gave to the love-commandments a more complete interpretation than did the Jewish lawyer! He refused to make an exception to the obligations of love, even in the case of a Jew. Here we have "a half-breed heretic fulfilling God's law better than the pillars of Jewry."[63]

The answer to the question, "Who is my neighbor?" that is given in the conduct of the Samaritan, is simple: "Who needs me is my neighbor."[64] It does not matter what the prejudices or bigotries of my own people, or of his people, may be. Nor does it matter what his race or color or

---

62. A. B. Bruce, The Parabolic Teaching of Christ, pp. 352-53.
63. Hunter, Interpreting the Parables, p. 73.
64. Oesterley, op. cit., p. 165.

beliefs or origin are. The basis of my obligation lies bluntly in the fact that he is also a man. "His neighbor is the human being, whoever he may be, with whom God brings him into contact, and who has need of his help."[65]

The average Samaritan would have said, "The Jews have no dealings with the Samaritans." The average Jew would have said, "No Samaritan, but only a fellow Jew, is my neighbor." But this was "a certain Samaritan," and the man in the roadside ditch was "a certain man." The service of love is a personal matter and not a general principle. The individual is responsible for obedience to the love-commandments in all the particularity of his own life. He cannot hide behind the neglect or corruption of that law that takes the shape of majority opinion.

Here was love acting in defiance and contradiction of the usually accepted boundaries. It was, in the words of A. B. Bruce, a love "stronger than fear . . . superior to prejudice . . . generous and uncalculating, grudging no expenditure of time, pains, or money. . . . In a word . . . a love like that of God's."[66]

3. The love that serves any man serves also every need of man

The love that Jesus describes in this story of the good Samaritan does not look upon men simply as souls to be saved. To the measure that his actions were prompted by the love-commandments contained in his own Scriptures, the help proffered by the Samaritan had a spiritual basis. But in the sort of things he did to express genuine, holy love, his help took a very practical form. He did not content himself to give a sign of sympathy and a promise to remember the

---

65. Godet, op. cit., p. 41.
66. *The Parabolic Teaching of Christ*, p. 347.

man in his prayers! He cleansed and assuaged his wounds, and took him to the first-century equivalent of a hospital. He was concerned to save his life, not simply his soul. He addressed his compassion to physical needs with material remedies.

This is not to deny for a moment that the deepest needs of men are spiritual, nor to deny that men need to be saved. But any attention we may hope for when we present the message of the gospel will certainly be forfeited if men are convinced that we care nothing for their whole persons.

Without endorsing the fanciful interpretations given by many ancient scholars who allegorized this story, we can nevertheless sympathize with their readiness to see Jesus himself as the Good Samaritan. It can be truly said that He draws a picture of love in action which was beautifully and supremely illustrated by His own life. He fed the hungry, healed the sick, cheered the despondent, and insisted that works of mercy would be an issue in the final judgment (cf. Matt. 25:31-46). Ignoring the threat of ceremonial defilement, He touched the leper's flesh. Scorning popular prejudice, He companied with social outcasts and notorious sinners. The love-commandments with which He summarized the entire law call upon men to love God with all the heart, soul, and mind, terms which "cover man's physical, intellectual, and moral activity."[67] The Lord was concerned to minister, therefore, to the needs of the whole man, physical, intellectual, and moral.

4. The life of service described in Jesus' teaching can spring only from transformed character

It is a gross misunderstanding of the parable of the good Samaritan that sees it as teaching that eternal life is

---

67. Godet, op. cit., p. 41.

won by doing good. Eternal life results from faith in Jesus Christ. To those who believe on Him the Lord gives life, His life, holy life. That freely given life enables us to love God and the neighbor. Such love for Him and for our fellow humans does not originate naturally but supernaturally. By nature we are prejudiced, bigoted, hating, and we live from selfish motives. Only by grace can we become like Him!

The parable answers the question asked, "Who is my neighbor?" And it answers the unasked question, What does it mean to love my neighbor? It was not an answer to the original question, "What shall I do to inherit eternal life?" and "therefore in no way implies that works of benevolence secure eternal life."[68] T. W. Manson is right in saying that the commandments to love are not enforceable. "They apply entirely to the disposition which man is to have towards God and his neighbor. . . . If the secret of good life lies in these two precepts, it lies in a change of heart, an inward transformation, the corollary to which is an outward reformation of behaviour. For Judaism good conduct is a part of religion; for Jesus it is a product of religion."[69]

That such transformation is possible we have already seen. The new birth, and the infilling with the Holy Spirit that cleanses from inner sin and fills the heart with love, provide the dynamic for the life of service. For any number of secondary motives men may do good works. But to serve men because you love God who made them, and to serve those who are unlike you and even enemies to you, this is possible only for those whom the Lord has transformed by grace.

* * *

---

68. Plummer, op. cit., p. 285.
69. Op. cit., p. 305.

The relevance of the passage to our preaching of holiness is obvious and challenging.

1. *We must preach service to human need, offered from motives of love, as the expression of genuine holiness.* The holiness of the New Testament is not a matter of private piety. The place of prayer, of fasting, of meditation, of self-examination is certainly recognized. So also is the place of worship and Christian fellowship. But the accent in Jesus' teaching falls upon love in action for the sake of others. Where Matthew speaks of being perfect, Luke speaks of being merciful. And in this parable "showed mercy" equals "loved his neighbor."

2. *We must preach love-inspired service that transcends the common prejudices and hatreds of our peers.* It is amazing and shocking that so much racial and class prejudice can exist among, and be rationalized within, holiness churches. At the risk of alienating those we love, we must be true to the message of the New Testament—that holiness is love embracing and serving even one's enemies! Holy love recognizes our common humanity with all others. When it finds a man suffering it does not ask, What is his color? or, What is his creed? or, What are his politics? or, What are my chances of being recompensed? It asks, How can I help?

3. *We must preach the purifying of the heart and the perfecting of love as the only adequate bases from which we may live as good Samaritans.* We know, from the Bible and from human experience, that the heart is prone to love its own little circle of friends and disregard others. We know that the outward deed is often marred by selfish motives. Self-centeredness is the very stuff of sin, defiling the heart and restricting the service. Only as the heart is cleansed from sin and filled with love can we consistently be like Christ in our ministries of helpfulness to people. Ours is the joyful responsibility of proclaiming that cleansing, of declaring

without stammering that Jesus has made ample and mighty provision, in His death and resurrection, to inwardly transform human life!

BIBLIOGRAPHY

Alford, Henry. *The Greek Testament.* London: Rivington's, 1859.

Baker's Dictionary of Theology. Edited by E. F. Harrison. Grand Rapids: Baker Book House, 1960.

Barclay, Wm. *The Beatitudes and the Lord's Prayer for Everyman.* New York: Harper & Row, 1964.

———. *The Daily Study Bible.* "The Gospel of Matthew." Philadelphia: Westminster Press, 1958.

Bonhoeffer, Dietrich. *The Cost of Discipleship.* New York: Macmillan Co., 1949.

Brown, David. *A Commentary Critical, Experimental, and Practical on the Old and New Testaments,* with Robert Jamieson and A. R. Fausset. Reprint. Grand Rapids: Wm. B. Eerdmans Publishing Co., 1948.

Bruce, A. B. *The Synoptic Gospels. The Expositor's Greek Testament,* Vol. 1. New York: Geo. H. Doran Co., n.d.

———. *The Parabolic Teaching of Christ.* New York: A. C. Armstrong and Son, 1908.

———. *The Training of the Twelve.* New York: A. C. Armstrong and Son, 1908.

Bruce, F. F. *Basic Christian Doctrines.* Edited by C. F. H. Henry. New York: Holt, Rinehart, & Winston, 1962.

———. *The New Testament Development of Old Testament Themes.* Grand Rapids: Wm. B. Eerdmans Publishing Co., 1968.

Calvin, John. *Commentary on a Harmony of the Evangelists.* Grand Rapids: Wm. B. Eerdmans Publishing Co., 1949.

Childers, Charles L. *Beacon Bible Commentary.* "Luke." Kansas City: Beacon Hill Press, 1964.

Companion to the Bible, A. Edited by J.-J. Von Allmen. New York: Oxford University Press, 1958.

Cowles, Henry. *Matthew and Mark.* New York: D. Appleton & Co., 1891.

Cox, G. E. P. *The Gospel According to St. Matthew.* Torch Bible Commentaries. London: SCM Press, 1952.

Cullmann, Oscar. *Christology of the New Testament.* Philadelphia: Westminster Press, 1959.

Earle, Ralph. *Beacon Bible Commentary.* "Matthew." Kansas City: Beacon Hill Press, 1964.

Eichrodt, Walther. *Theology of the Old Testament.* 2 vols. Philadelphia: Westminster Press, 1961-67.

Ellison, H. L. *A New Testament Commentary.* "The Gospel According to Matthew." Edited by G. C. D. Howley. Grand Rapids: Zondervan Publishing House, 1969.

Filson, Floyd. *A Commentary on the Gospel According to St. Matthew.* New York: Harper & Brothers, 1960.

Flew, R. Newton. *Jesus and His Way.* London: Epworth Press, 1963.

Geldenhuys, Norval. *Commentary on the Gospel of Luke.* New International Commentary on the New Testament. Grand Rapids: Wm. B. Eerdmans Publishing Co., 1956.

Gingrich, F. Wilbur. *Shorter Lexicon of the Greek New Testament.* Chicago: University of Chicago Press, 1965.

Godet, F. L. *Commentary on the Gospel of Luke.* Classic Commentary Library. Reprint. Grand Rapids: Zondervan Publishing House, n.d.

Gould, J. Glenn. *The Whole Counsel of God.* Kansas City: Beacon Hill Press, 1945.

Grant, F. C. *The Gospel of Mark.* Harper's Annotated Bible Series. New York: Harper & Brothers, 1952.

Harrison, E. F. *A Short Life of Christ.* Grand Rapids: Wm. B. Eerdmans Publishing Co., 1968.

Hunter, A. M. *A Pattern for Life.* Philadelphia: Westminster Press, 1965.

———. *Interpreting the Parables.* Philadelphia: Westminster Press, 1960.

———. *The Gospel According to Saint Mark.* Torch Bible Commentaries. London: SCM Press, 1965.

International Standard Bible Encyclopaedia, The. Edited by James Orr. Chicago: Howard-Severance Co., 1915.

Jeremias, Joachim. *The Parables of Jesus.* New York: Charles Scribner's Sons, 1963.

Leaney, A. R. C. *A Commentary on the Gospel According to St. Luke.* Harper's New Testament Commentaries. New York: Harper & Brothers, 1958.

Linnemann, Eta. *Parables of Jesus.* London: SPCK, 1966.

Lohmeyer, Ernst. *"Our Father."* New York: Harper & Row, 1965.

Machen, J. Gresham. *The Virgin Birth of Christ.* Grand Rapids: Baker Book House, 1965.

Manson, T. W. *The Teaching of Jesus.* Cambridge: The University Press, 1948.

Morgan, G. Campbell. *The Crises of the Christ.* New York: Fleming H. Revell Co., 1936.

———. *The Parables and Metaphors of Our Lord.* New York: Fleming H. Revell Co., 1943.

———. *The Voice of the Devil.* New York: Fleming H. Revell Co., n.d.

Oesterley, W. O. E. *The Gospel Parables in the Light of Their Jewish Backgrounds.* London: SPCK, 1936.

Plummer, Alfred. *A Critical and Exegetical Commentary on the Gospel According to St. Luke.* The International Critical Commentary. Edinburgh: T. & T. Clark, 1910.

Rowley, H. H. *The Faith of Israel.* Philadelphia: Westminster Press, 1956.

Simcox, C. E. *The First Gospel.* Greenwich, Conn.: Seabury Press, 1963.

Spicq, Ceslaus. *Agape in the New Testament.* St. Louis: B. Herder Book Co., 1963.

Stagg, Frank, *The Broadman Bible Commentary.* "Matthew." Nashville: Broadman Press, 1969.

Tasker, R. V. G. *The Gospel According to St. Matthew.* Tyndale Bible Commentaries. Grand Rapids: Wm. B. Eerdmans Publishing Co., 1961.

Taylor, Vincent. *The Life and Ministry of Jesus*. New York: Abingdon Press, n.d.

———. *The Name of Jesus*. London: Macmillan & Co., 1954.

Theological Dictionary of the New Testament. Edited by Gerhard Kittel. Translated and edited by Geoffrey W. Bromiley. Grand Rapids: Wm. B. Eerdmans Publishing Co., 1964.

Varillon, Francois. *Announcing Christ*. Westminster, Md.: Newman Press, 1964.

Vriezen, Th. C. *An Outline of Old Testament Theology*. Wageningen, Holland: H. Veenman & Zonen, N. V., 1960.

Wesley, John. *A Plain Account of Christian Perfection*. Reprint. Kansas City: Beacon Hill Press of Kansas City, 1966.